Noodles

MILK STREET

Noodles

CHRISTOPHER KIMBALL

WRITING AND EDITING BY

J. M. Hirsch, Michelle Locke and Dawn Yanagihara

RECIPES BY

Wes Martin, Diane Unger, Bianca Borges, Matthew Card
and the Cooks at Milk Street

ART DIRECTION BY

Jennifer Baldino Cox and Gabriella Rinaldo

PHOTOGRAPHY BY

Connie Miller of CB Creatives

STYLING BY

Catrine Kelty

VORACIOUS

LITTLE, BROWN AND COMPANY

NEW YORK BOSTON LONDON

Voracious / Little, Brown and Company
Hachette Book Group
1290 Avenue of the Americas, New York, NY 10104
littlebrown.com

First edition: April 2023

Voracious is an imprint of Little, Brown and Company, a division of Hachette Book Group, Inc.

The Voracious name and logo are trademarks of Hachette Book Group, Inc.

The Hachette Speakers Bureau provides a wide range of authors for speaking events. To find out more, go to hachettespeakersbureau.com or call (866) 376-6591.

Voracious / Little, Brown and Company books may be purchased in bulk for business, educational, or promotional use. For information, please contact your local bookseller or the Hachette Book Group Special Markets Department at special.markets@hbgusa.com.

Photography Credits: Connie Miller of CB Creatives
Behind the Scenes photography by Gabriella Rinaldo
Author photograph by Channing Johnson

ISBN 9780316387767
LCCN 2022941818

10 9 8 7 6 5 4 3 2 1

IM

Print book interior design by Gary Tooth / Empire Design Studio

Contents

Noodle Soups 61

Fast & Saucy 91

Italian Classics 135

Stir-Fries 169

One-Pan Pastas   199

Hearty Pastas 243

Index 274

Acknowledgments 284

Introduction

Sonoko Sakai, author of *Japanese Home Cooking*, was jumping up and down in stocking feet on a bag of udon noodle dough, her preferred approach to kneading. I followed her lead, having just put on the bright orange socks she purchased for me for the occasion.

We then moved into her sunny kitchen in the Highland Park neighborhood of East Los Angeles, where the dough was transformed into udon noodles using a special noodle knife akin to a Chinese cleaver. The noodles were briefly cooked and served with a spicy meat and mushroom sauce for lunch. Heaven.

What was not lost on me is that udon noodles are made from just three ingredients: flour, water and salt. Other noodles incorporate eggs, while still others may substitute olive oil for water. But the notion remains the same—the world over, noodles are a simple combination of ingredients transformed into thousands of shapes, recipes and uses. It's the perfect food and it's at home from Japan to Peru, and from Italy to India to China.

Beyond the classic Italian plate of spaghetti tossed with ragù or pesto, there is an almost infinite universe of recipes, from ramen to Spaetzle, from lo mein to gnocchi, from couscous to fregola. Like chicken soup, noodles are a cultural litmus test of sorts, bringing to the fore the flavors, techniques and preferences that make every culture special and captivating.

And, we need no reminder, noodles are the ultimate fast food. How many evenings have I quick-boiled a batch of soba or udon, topped them with leftover chicken or steamed vegetables, then finished them with a sauce of soy, mirin, sesame oil and perhaps a dash of oyster sauce? There's dinner in minutes.

But I always return to my visit with Sonoko Sakai. Her udon noodles tell a story of a place, of a culture, of how simple ingredients are transformed into shared experience and history.

And that is the charm of noodles. They have a past. They have a future. And they charm and delight in almost every kitchen in the world.

Where to
Use Your Noodles

Tagliatelle

Udon

Vermicelli

Whole-Wheat Linguine

Ziti

Pasta Primer

Asian Noodles

China is home to the world's oldest known noodles, a bowl of slender, yellow strands about 4,000 years old that were unearthed at an excavation site near the Yellow River. Modern-day Asian noodles typically are made from wheat or rice, though there also are varieties made from yam and mung beans. They may be chewy, soft, springy, dried or fresh. Wheat-based Asian noodles aren't made of the hard durum wheat typical of Italian pasta and, therefore, cook more quickly. Some require rinsing after cooking to remove excess starch, and all are cooked in unsalted water. They should be cooked until tender—not al dente. Tasting for doneness is the best way to know when your noodles are ready.

A RUNDOWN:

Asian Wheat Noodles

Wheat noodles comprise a broad category, but when we refer to fresh Asian wheat noodles we generally mean varieties that are about the size of spaghetti. They're great in stir-fries or simply sauced. Fresh Asian noodles are often sold in the refrigerated section of the supermarket, near the tofu. Dried Asian wheat noodles, in particular lo mein, are also a good and often more widely available option.

Glass Noodles

Glass noodles are thin and wiry and are sometimes called cellophane noodles, bean threads or sai fun. Made of vegetable starch, usually mung bean, they turn translucent when cooked. Typical prep is a 15-minute soak in boiling water.

Ramen

Chewy and stretchy, ramen are made of wheat flour and an alkaline solution that gives the noodles their yellow hue and springy texture. They usually are eaten in brothy soups or stir-fried with vegetables and are most commonly sold in the U.S. in instant form, but also available fresh, frozen and dried. We lean toward dried, non-instant ramen, because it's easier to source than fresh. The noodles, which might be straight like spaghetti or squiggly and formed into a slab, cook in about 4 minutes. Drain and rinse in cold water, or drain and immediately add to soup. Don't have any ramen on hand? We show you how to "ramenize" Italian pasta using just water and baking soda, see p. 179.

Rice Sticks

Different from thin rice sticks, these are ribbon-like noodles, sold in widths ranging from ⅛ to ½ inch, used for dishes such as pad Thai and pho. They're made of rice flour and are most commonly sold dried. To prepare them for stir-frying, the noodles are usually first softened by a soak in hot water or, in the case of soups, they are quickly cooked in boiling water.

Rice Vermicelli

Also known as thin rice sticks or maifun, these are thin, wiry noodles used in soups, salads and stir-fries. Don't confuse them with wide, flat rice sticks used in pad Thai or pho.

Soba

Gray-brown and nutty, soba is made from buckwheat flour or a blend of buckwheat and wheat flour. It sometimes is flavored with matcha (green tea powder) to make cha soba. Usually served chilled with a

Hand-Cut Wheat Noodles p. 9

dashi-soy dipping sauce, or hot, in a dashi-based broth, though we also like them in noodle salads. They are sold dried and fresh (frozen). We prefer the clean, nutty flavor of dried 100 percent buckwheat soba, but this type can be difficult to find. Cook for 7 to 8 minutes, or until tender. Drain and rinse with cold water.

Somen
Delicate, pale and thin, somen are made from wheat flour dough that is oiled, then stretched several times. The noodles, sold dried, packaged in bundles, usually are served chilled in summer months with a soy-based sauce or dressing or dipping sauce. Add to boiling water and cook for 2 or 3 minutes, stirring gently to prevent sticking, then drain and rinse with cold water.

Sweet Potato Noodles (Dang Myun)
Some recipes refer to these as glass noodles, but these Korean noodles are quite different, and are made, as the name implies, from sweet potato starch. They are grayish brown in color, uniquely springy, and translucent when cooked. They have the ability to really soak up flavors and are often used in soups and stir-fries.

Udon
Chewy and well-kneaded udon are a Japanese noodle made from wheat flour, water and salt and prepared in a variety of thicknesses. They are served hot in soup, stir-fried or chilled with dipping sauce, and are sold dried, frozen and fresh (refrigerated and shelf-stable). We prefer the firm, springy texture of frozen udon, which is already cooked, but dried udon is easier to source. Boil until tender, then drain and rinse with cold water to stop cooking.

Homemade Udon Noodles

Start to finish: 4 hours (1½ hours active)
Makes about 1¾ pounds uncooked noodles (about 3 pounds cooked noodles)

Udon is a type of Japanese wheat noodle. The thick, chewy strands can be served in hot soup, eaten cold with dipping sauce, stir-fried or simply sauced. When adapting Sonoko Sakai's udon formula from her book, "Japanese Home Cooking," we found that the brand of flour used and relative humidity can impact how much water is needed to make the noodle dough. For best results, the dough should be on the dry side and should contain just enough moisture so it holds together shaggily; if needed, work in more water 1 tablespoon at a time, but err on the side of dry rather than wet. With resting and kneading, the dough will hydrate and become smooth, silky and elastic. The classic way to knead dough for udon is to stomp on it by foot, a good—and fun!—way to develop strong gluten structure; we put the dough in a doubled heavy-duty plastic bag before stepping on it (without shoes, of course) to ensure everything stays clean. If you find the dough is difficult to roll because of its elasticity, allow it intermittent rests. You can alternate between the two pieces, rolling one while the other relaxes. Aim for a ⅛-inch thickness so the noodles aren't too thick; they expand when boiled. Unlike most fresh noodles, this udon requires lengthy cooking—about 15 minutes of boiling—to attain the correct texture.

1½ tablespoons table salt	4 cups all-purpose flour
1 cup warm water (about 100°F)	Cornstarch, for dusting

In a small bowl or a measuring cup, mix together the salt and warm water until the salt dissolves. Put the flour in a large bowl, add half of the salt water and mix with a wooden spoon until the water is absorbed. Add the remaining saltwater and mix, using your hands once the water has been absorbed, until a very shaggy dough forms. If the mixture is very dry and won't come together, mix in additional water 1 tablespoon at a time, but it's better to err on the side of too little water than too much. Transfer to a 1-gallon heavy-duty zip-close bag, press out the air and partially seal the bag; let rest for 30 minutes.

Place the bag with the dough inside another 1-gallon zip-close bag, press out the air and partially seal. Lay the bag on the floor and repeatedly step on the dough with your feet, being careful not to tear or puncture the

01

02

03

04

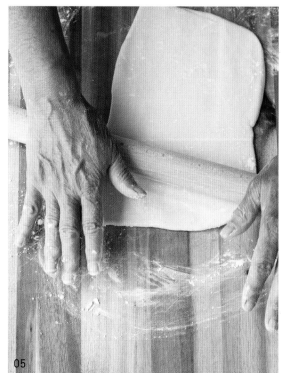

05

plastic, until the dough is flattened and fills the bag to the edges. Remove the dough from the bag and set it on the counter. Fold it into thirds like a business letter, return it to the inner bag and partially seal both bags. Repeat the process 4 more times, until the dough is very smooth and elastic; after the fifth pressing, leave the dough flat (do not fold it into thirds). Seal the bags and let the dough rest at room temperature for at least 1 hour or refrigerate for up to 1 day (if refrigerated, let the dough stand at room temperature for about 1 hour before proceeding).

Lightly dust a rimmed baking sheet and the counter with cornstarch. Remove the dough from the bags and set it on the counter. Using a chef's knife, cut the dough in half. Return one piece to the inner bag and seal it. Using a rolling pin, roll out the second piece until it is ⅛ inch thick. The shape of the rolled dough doesn't matter; it's more important that the dough be of an even thickness. Dust the surface of the dough with cornstarch, then accordion-fold the dough into thirds; set it on a cutting board. Using a chef's knife and a decisive cutting motion (do not use a sawing action), cut the dough crosswise into ⅛-inch-wide noodles. Unfold the noodles and transfer them to the prepared baking sheet, gently separating them; toss to lightly coat with cornstarch and cover with a kitchen towel. Roll and cut the remaining dough in the same way.

In a large (at least 8-quart) pot, bring 5 quarts water to a boil. Using your hands, add the noodles to the pot, first shaking them over the baking sheet to remove excess starch. Cook, stirring occasionally, until a noodle rinsed under cold water is tender, 10 to 15 minutes. Drain in a colander, rinse the noodles under cold running water and drain again.

06

07

Hand-Cut Wheat Noodles

Start to finish: 1 hour (35 minutes active)
Makes about 1 pound uncooked noodles

These Asian-style wheat noodles can be simply sauced or used in a wide variety of soups and stir-fries. The dough comes together easily and, once rolled, can be cut with a knife into noodles of the desired width, from slender linguine-like strands to ribbons about ½ inch wide. If the noodles end up slightly uneven, not to worry—it adds to their charm. We use bread flour to make a strong, gluten-rich dough that handles beautifully and cooks up into noodles with a satisfyingly springy texture, no matter their thickness or width. With each step of rolling and cutting, be sure to dust the dough with flour to prevent the noodles from sticking together. But at the stovetop, be sure to shake off excess flour as you add the noodles to the boiling water. After draining the noodles, rinse them under running water to remove excess starch.

1 tablespoon grapeseed
or other neutral oil

2 cups bread flour, plus
more for dusting

½ teaspoon table salt

In a small bowl or liquid measuring cup, combine ½ cup water and the oil. In a medium bowl, whisk together the flour and salt. Make a well in the center, then add the liquid. Using a fork, stir in a circular motion, starting in the center and gradually moving outward to incorporate the wet and dry ingredients, until a shaggy dough forms. Using the heel of your palm, begin kneading the dough, swiping along the edges of the bowl to incorporate any dry bits. If the dough resists coming together, add more water, a few drops at a time, until all the flour is just moistened. Knead in the bowl until the dough is smooth and cohesive, about 10 minutes.

01

02

03

Lightly dust the counter with flour and turn the dough out onto it; knead until soft and springy, about 10 minutes. Form into a ball, cover with plastic wrap and let rest at room temperature for at least 20 minutes or up to 1 hour.

Line a rimmed baking sheet with a kitchen towel and lightly dust with flour. Lightly flour the counter and set the dough on the floured surface. Using a rolling pin and dusting with flour as needed to prevent sticking, roll the dough to an even ⅛- to ¹⁄₁₆-inch thickness. (If the dough sheet winds up longer than 16 to 18 inches, cut in half crosswise for slightly shorter lengths.) Dust the surface of the dough with flour, then accordion-fold it into thirds, sprinkling flour between each fold; set it on a cutting board. Using a chef's knife and a decisive cutting motion (do not use a sawing action), cut the dough crosswise into strips of the desired width. Unfold the noodles and transfer to the prepared baking sheet, gently separating the strands. Dust with flour and toss to lightly coat. If making ahead, cover with plastic wrap and refrigerate for up to 24 hours.

To cook the noodles, follow the directions in the recipe that you are making, or in a large pot, bring 4 quarts water to a boil. Add the noodles, first shaking them over the baking sheet to remove excess flour. Cook, stirring occasionally, until the noodles are tender, about 5 minutes for thin noodles or up to about 8 minutes for wider ones. Drain, rinse under cold water and drain again.

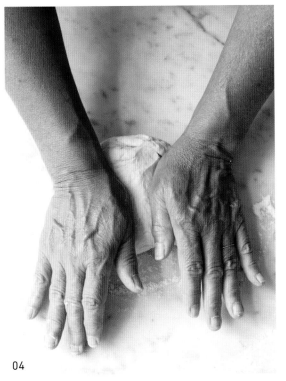

04

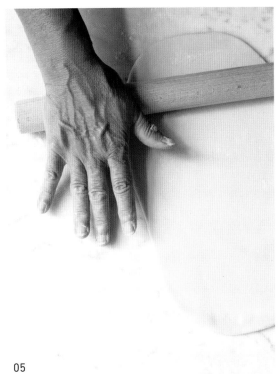

05

06

07

Italian Pasta

Italian dried pasta is made with durum semolina and generally is designed to be cooked to al dente texture, literally "to the tooth," meaning still with a bit of bite to it. In dishes where the pasta finishes cooking in a sauce, we often stop the pasta cooking just short of al dente. The final simmer in the sauce finishes the pasta while giving it a chance to absorb flavor. Italian cuisine boasts hundreds of different takes on pasta—short, long, filled, plain or intricately shaped—and just as many ways to serve it.

A RUNDOWN:

Bucatini

Looks like fat spaghetti but has a hole in the center, the better for sucking up sauces. This is a good noodle to use when the dish is all about the sauce.

Capellini

Also known as angel hair. Long and thin, this cooks quickly and is good with light sauces and in soups.

Ditalini

Small and tubular, this is an excellent soup noodle though it also fares well in salads.

Farfalle

Also known as bow-tie pasta, the name comes from the Italian word for butterflies. The shape makes this pasta a fun addition to salads—green and red options can often be found—and the ruffled edges make farfalle good at catching bits of sauce.

Fettuccine

Literally named "little ribbons," this long, flat pasta is popular in Tuscan and Roman cooking and is indelibly associated with the dish known as fettuccine Alfredo. Interestingly, though this can be an over-the-top arterial assault in the U.S., we were served a still-delicious but light version in Rome made of just fresh pasta, Parmigiano Reggiano cheese, butter and salt, see recipe p. 143.

Fregola

Fregola sarda is a small bead-shaped pasta from Sardinia. The fregola is toasted until golden brown and nutty, which makes it chewier—almost meaty in texture—and more resilient than standard pasta. Fregola is sold in Italian markets. If not available, toasted pearl couscous is a good substitute.

Fusilli

This corkscrew-shaped short pasta is excellent at catching bits of sauce. We like to use it in just about any recipe calling for short pasta.

Gnocchi

Gnocchi is more of a dumpling than a noodle, depending on how it's made. Potato gnocchi falls in dumpling territory, made simply of mashed potato with a little flour and egg with herbs or other seasonings mixed in. There's also gnocchi di farina (farina meaning flour) made of just flour, water and salt, an excellent example of "la cucina povera," simple and satisfying.

Fresh egg pasta p. 15

Lasagna

Wide and flat, lasagna (plural lasagne) may be one of the older forms of pasta; it's referenced in medieval writings. Today, it's the centerpiece of the dish known as lasagna, a comforting mix of noodle, sauce, meat and/or vegetables and plenty of cheese.

Orecchiette

Orecchiette means "little ears," and this pasta's cup-like shape is ideal for catching sauce.

Orzo

Orzo means barley in Italian, and this very small pasta looks like rice. But confusing nomenclature aside, this pasta (not made of barley) is a good addition to soups, adding a bit—but not too much—heft. It's also good toasted and used in salads.

Penne

Penne translates from the Italian as "feather." The short tubes are cut at an angle, resulting in points that resemble a quill nib. Regular penne is smooth; penne rigate has a ridged exterior. Either works especially well with chunky sauces.

Spaghetti

Spaghetti's long, round strands combine well with smooth or creamy sauces, but also are a good match for chunkier ragùs. It can be a stand-in for some types of Asian noodles.

Ziti

Short and hollow, tube-like ziti typically is used in baked pasta dishes.

Fresh Egg Pasta

Start to finish: 40 minutes, plus resting
Makes 1 pound pasta

To make these luxurious, golden-hued noodles, we use a fairly large number of egg yolks plus a whole egg, along with all-purpose flour and just a small amount of water. Determining the right amount of eggs is a balancing act—too many and the dough becomes difficult to roll out, as the fat in the yolks disrupts the formation of gluten. But too few and the dough will lack the desired richness. Given multiple passes through a pasta machine to produce long, thin sheets, the dough can be filled and made into ravioli, tortellini or other stuffed shapes, or it can be cut into fettuccine, tagliatelle or pappardelle as instructed in the directions. If you don't own a pasta machine but are skilled with a rolling pin, the dough can be rolled into sheets by hand. This homemade pasta is especially good with hearty ragù Bolognese (see recipe p. 146) and shines when made into elegantly delicate fettuccine Alfredo (see recipe p. 143).

1 large whole egg,
plus 7 large egg yolks

2 cups all-purpose flour,
plus more for dusting

Kosher salt, for cooking

In a 2-cup liquid measuring cup or small bowl, beat together the whole egg, egg yolks and 2 tablespoons water.

To make the dough in a food processor: Put the flour in a food processor. With the processor running, slowly stream in the egg mixture. Process until the dough leaves the sides of the bowl in large chunks, 1 to 2 minutes. If the dough feels dry and doesn't hold together when pinched, add water, 1 teaspoon at a time, as needed. If the dough feels sticky, you will have the chance to knead in more flour after turning the dough out onto the counter.

To make the dough by hand: Put the flour in a large bowl and make a well in the center. Add the egg mixture; using a fork, stir the flour into the eggs, working from the outside edges into the center, until all of the flour is incorporated. Form into a rough ball. If the dough feels dry and doesn't hold together when pinched, add water, 1 teaspoon at a time, as needed. If the dough feels sticky, you will have the chance to knead in more flour after turning the dough out onto the counter.

Lightly dust the counter with flour; if the dough feels wet and sticky, apply a heavier layer of flour to the work surface. Turn the dough out onto it and knead until smooth and shiny, 5 to 10 minutes. Press a finger into the surface of the dough; it should bounce back quickly, within 2 seconds. Cover the dough with a kitchen towel or plastic wrap and let rest at room temperature for 1 hour, or wrap tightly in plastic wrap and refrigerate up to 24 hours.

Line a rimmed baking sheet with a kitchen towel and lightly dust with flour. If the dough has been refrigerated, let it stand, still wrapped in plastic, at room temperature for about 15 minutes before proceeding.

Uncover or unwrap the dough and cut it into quarters. Set 3 pieces aside and cover with plastic wrap. Shape the remaining piece into a rough 4-by-6-inch rectangle. Using a pasta machine or a stand mixer fitted with a pasta attachment, roll the dough through several times, gradually reducing the thickness setting on the machine,

01

02

03

04

05

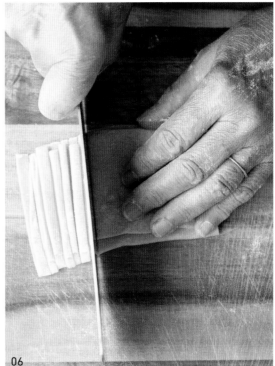

06

until it forms a long sheet about ¹⁄₁₆ inch thick. It's important that the dough be of an even thickness. If the pasta sheet is longer than 14 inches, cut in half for slightly shorter lengths.

Dust the surface of the dough with flour, then accordion-fold it into thirds; set it on a cutting board. Using a chef's knife and a decisive cutting motion (do not use a sawing action), cut the dough crosswise into ¼-inch-wide strips for tagliatelle or fettuccine, up to ½ inch wide for pappardelle. Unfold the pasta and transfer to the prepared baking sheet, gently separating the strands, then toss to lightly coat with flour; keep uncovered. Roll and cut the remaining dough in the same way. If not cooking right away, dust with additional flour and keep uncovered at room temperature for up to 1 hour, or cover with a kitchen towel and refrigerate for up to 12 hours.

To cook the noodles, follow the directions in the pasta recipe that you are making, or in a large pot, bring 4 quarts water to a boil. Add 1 tablespoon salt and the pasta, then cook, stirring occasionally, until al dente. Reserve some of the cooking water if directed in your recipe, then drain the pasta.

07

Fresh Saffron Pasta

Start to finish: 40 minutes, plus resting
Makes 1 pound pasta

In the Italian kitchen, saffron is perhaps best known as the flavoring in risotto Milanese. But the prized spice also is a wonderful complement to homemade pasta. So we infuse our fresh egg pasta dough with saffron threads, which lends a floral aroma, subtly earthy flavor and rich golden tint. To fully release its flavor and aroma, we first crush the saffron, then bloom it in warm water before adding it to the dough. Toss this luscious pasta with a simple cream sauce or use it as a bed for poached scallops or lobster.

½ teaspoon saffron
threads, crumbled

1 large whole egg,
plus 7 large egg yolks

2 cups all-purpose flour,
plus more for dusting

Kosher salt, for cooking

In a small microwave-safe bowl, combine the saffron and 2 tablespoons water. Microwave on high until the water takes on a reddish hue, about 30 seconds. Stir, then cool until barely warm to the touch, about 5 minutes.

In a 2-cup liquid measuring cup or small bowl, beat together the whole egg, egg yolks and the saffron-infused water.

To make the dough in a food processor: Put the flour in a food processor. With the processor running, slowly stream in the egg mixture. Process until the dough leaves the sides of the bowl in large chunks, 1 to 2 minutes. If the dough feels dry and doesn't hold together when pinched, add water, 1 teaspoon at a time, as needed. If the dough feels sticky, you will have the chance to knead in more flour after turning the dough out onto the counter.

To make the dough by hand: Put the flour in a large bowl and make a well in the center. Add the egg mixture; using a fork, stir the flour into the eggs, working from the outside edges into the center, until all of the flour is incorporated. Form into a rough ball. If the dough feels dry and doesn't hold together when pinched, add water, 1 teaspoon at a time, as needed. If the dough feels sticky, you will have the chance to knead in more flour after turning the dough out onto the counter.

Lightly dust the counter with flour; if the dough feels wet and sticky, apply a heavier layer of flour to the work surface. Turn the dough out onto it and knead until smooth and shiny, 5 to 10 minutes. Press a finger into the surface of the dough; it should bounce back quickly, within 2 seconds. Cover the dough with a kitchen towel or plastic wrap and let rest at room temperature for 1 hour, or wrap tightly in plastic wrap and refrigerate for up to 24 hours.

Line a rimmed baking sheet with a kitchen towel and lightly dust with flour. If the dough has been refrigerated, let it stand, still wrapped in plastic, at room temperature for about 15 minutes before proceeding.

Uncover or unwrap the dough and, using a knife, cut it into quarters. Set 3 pieces aside and cover with plastic wrap. Shape the remaining piece into a rough 4-by-6-inch rectangle. Using a pasta machine or a stand mixer fitted with a pasta attachment, roll the dough through several times, gradually reducing the thickness setting on the machine, until it forms a long sheet about 1/16 inch thick. It's important that the dough be of an even thickness. If the pasta sheet is longer than 14 inches, cut in half for slightly shorter lengths.

Dust the surface of the dough with flour, then accordion-fold it into thirds; set it on a cutting board. Using a chef's knife and a decisive cutting motion (do not use a sawing action), cut the dough crosswise into 1/4-inch-wide strips

for tagliatelle or fettuccine, up to 1/2 inch wide for pappardelle. Unfold the pasta and transfer to the prepared baking sheet, gently separating the strands, then toss to lightly coat with flour; keep uncovered. Roll and cut the remaining dough in the same way. If not cooking right away, dust with additional flour and keep uncovered at room temperature for up to 1 hour, or cover with a kitchen towel and refrigerate for up to 12 hours.

To cook the noodles, follow the directions in the pasta recipe that you are making, or in a large pot, bring 4 quarts water to a boil. Add 1 tablespoon salt and the pasta, then cook, stirring occasionally, until al dente. Reserve some of the cooking water if directed in your recipe, then drain the pasta.

Fresh Herb Pasta

Start to finish: 40 minutes, plus resting
Makes 1 pound pasta

This recipe enhances homemade egg pasta by incorporating fresh herbs, which give the dough a lovely green hue and lend bright flavor to each bite. We use dill and chives, which are assertive enough to hold up to the richness of an abundance of egg yolks. For a milder option, swap in parsley for the dill. The dough needs to be prepared in a food processor, rather than by hand, as the processor will chop the herbs finely and incorporate them evenly into the flour mixture. This pasta is delicious tossed with an Alfredo sauce or finished with smoked salmon. Or serve the noodles simply, drizzled with olive oil or melted butter and sprinkled with lemon juice and Parmesan.

1 large whole egg, plus 7 large egg yolks

2 cups all-purpose flour, plus more for dusting

1 cup lightly packed fresh dill or 2 cups lightly packed fresh flat-leaf parsley

¼ cup chopped fresh chives

Kosher salt, for cooking

In a 2-cup liquid measuring cup or small bowl, beat together the whole egg, egg yolks and 2 tablespoons water.

In a food processor, combine the flour, dill and chives. Process until the herbs are in fine bits and fully incorporated into the flour, about 30 seconds. With the processor running, slowly stream in the egg mixture. Process until the dough leaves the sides of the bowl in large chunks, 1 to 2 minutes. If the dough feels dry and doesn't hold together when pinched, add water, 1 teaspoon at a time, as needed. If the dough feels sticky, you will have the chance to knead in more flour after turning the dough out onto the counter.

Lightly dust the counter with flour; if the dough feels wet and sticky, apply a heavier layer of flour to the work surface. Turn the dough out onto it and knead until smooth and shiny, 5 to 10 minutes. Press a finger into the surface of the dough; it should bounce back quickly, within 2 seconds. Cover the dough with a kitchen towel or plastic wrap and let rest at room temperature for 1 hour, or wrap tightly in plastic wrap and refrigerate for up to 24 hours.

Line a rimmed baking sheet with a kitchen towel and lightly dust with flour. If the dough has been refrigerated, let it stand, still wrapped in plastic, at room temperature for about 15 minutes before proceeding.

Uncover or unwrap the dough and, using a knife, cut it into quarters. Set 3 pieces aside and cover with plastic wrap. Shape the remaining piece into a rough 4-by-6-inch rectangle. Using a pasta machine or a stand mixer fitted with a pasta attachment, roll the dough through several times, gradually reducing the thickness setting on the machine, until it forms a long sheet about 1/16 inch thick. It's important that the dough be of an even thickness. If the pasta sheet is longer than 14 inches, cut in half for slightly shorter lengths.

Dust the surface of the dough with flour, then accordion-fold it into thirds; set it on a cutting board. Using a chef's knife and a decisive cutting motion (do not use a sawing action), cut the dough crosswise into ¼-inch-wide strips for tagliatelle or fettuccine, up to ½ inch wide for pappardelle. Unfold the pasta and transfer to the prepared baking sheet, gently separating the strands, then toss to lightly coat with flour; keep uncovered. Roll and cut the remaining dough in the same way. If not cooking right away, dust with additional flour and keep uncovered at room temperature for up to 1 hour, or cover with a kitchen towel and refrigerate for up to 12 hours.

To cook the noodles, follow the directions in the pasta recipe that you are making, or in a large pot, bring 4 quarts water to a boil. Add 1 tablespoon salt and the pasta, then cook, stirring occasionally, until al dente. Reserve some of the cooking water if directed in your recipe, then drain the pasta.

Potato Gnocchi

Start to finish: 1¾ hours, plus cooling
Makes about 2 pounds, serving 4 to 6

Our take on classic potato gnocchi was informed by a hands-on cooking lesson from Australian chef Peter Orr when he was proprietor of Robert, his former restaurant in Paris' 11th arrondissement. Weighing the potatoes on a kitchen scale after cooking and draining is the best way to ensure the right quantity is used in the dough. The gnocchi can be cooked, cooled completely on the wire rack, then transferred to a baking sheet that has been lined with parchment and misted with cooking spray; cover with plastic wrap and refrigerate for up to 24 hours. For longer storage, after covering with plastic, freeze until solid, about two hours, then transfer to a zip-close bag and freeze for up to a month. To thaw, spread the dumplings in an even layer on a lightly oiled baking sheet and let stand at room temperature until soft to the touch, about one hour. Heat the chilled or thawed gnocchi by adding them to sauce that is already hot, tossing with a silicone spatula until warmed.

2 pounds russet potatoes, peeled and cut into 1-inch chunks	1 cup plus 2 tablespoons all-purpose flour, plus more for shaping
Kosher salt	½ teaspoon baking powder
	1 large egg, lightly beaten

In a large pot, combine the potatoes and 4 quarts water. Bring to a boil over high, then stir in 1 tablespoon salt. Reduce to medium-high and cook, stirring occasionally, until the potatoes break apart when pierced with a knife, 15 to 20 minutes. Meanwhile, set a wire rack in a rimmed baking sheet and line another baking sheet with kitchen parchment.

Drain the potatoes in a colander, shaking the colander to remove excess water. Transfer the potatoes to the prepared rack in an even layer, then cool to room temperature. Meanwhile, in a small bowl, whisk together the flour, baking powder and 1 teaspoon salt.

Weigh out 1¼ pounds (about 4 cups) of the cooled cooked potatoes into a large bowl; save the remainder for another use. Reserve the rack and the baking sheet for cooling the cooked gnocchi. Pass the potatoes through a ricer or a food mill fitted with the fine disk back into the bowl, or mash them with a potato masher until smooth.

Sprinkle the flour mixture evenly over the mashed potatoes. Using your hands, lightly toss the potatoes to distribute the flour mixture. Add the egg and gently mix with your hands until incorporated. Turn the dough out onto a lightly floured counter and gently knead just until smooth; do not over knead.

Using a bench scraper, divide the dough into 4 pieces and cover with a kitchen towel. Using your hands, roll one piece of dough against the counter into a rope about 18 inches long and about ¾ inch in diameter. Cut the rope into ½-inch pieces and lightly dust the pieces with flour. Dip the back of the tines of a fork into flour, then gently press into each piece to create a ridged surface. Transfer the gnocchi to the parchment-lined baking sheet; try to not allow them to touch. Shape the remaining pieces of dough in the same way.

In a large pot, bring 4 quarts water to a boil. Add 1 tablespoon salt followed by about a third of the gnocchi. Return to a boil, stirring once or twice, and cook for 2 minutes (the gnocchi will float to the surface even before they are cooked through). Using a slotted spoon and allowing excess water to fall back into the pot, transfer the gnocchi to the prepared rack; spread them out so they don't touch. The gnocchi will be very soft at this point,

but will firm up as they cool. Return the water to a boil, then cook and drain the remaining gnocchi in the same way, in two more batches.

After the final batch of gnocchi has been transferred to the rack, reserve cooking water as needed for saucing; discard the remainder. Let the gnocchi cool for at least 10 minutes or up to 1 hour to allow them to firm up.

01

02

03

04

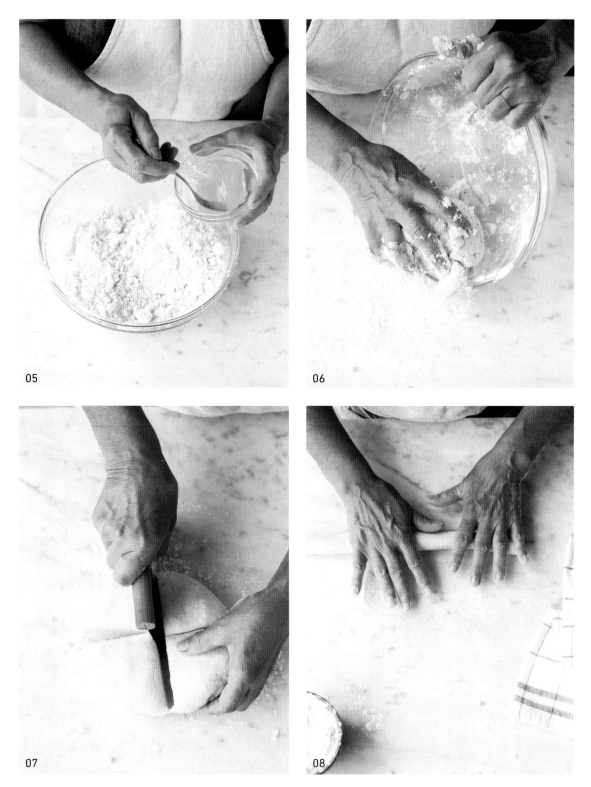

05

06

07

08

Gnocchi di Farina

Start to finish: 1 hour, plus cooling
Makes about 2 pounds, serving 4 to 6

Gnocchi made with potatoes are undoubtedly the best-known variety of the light, tender Italian dumplings. But gnocchi di farina are simpler to prepare and, arguably, equally delicious. Farina is Italian for "flour," and these gnocchi di farina are made with nothing more than flour, water and salt. This is our adaptation of the recipe we learned from Antonio Cioffi, chef at La Vecchia Cantina in Naples. The gnocchi can be prepared and cooked in advance, ready to be finished with your favorite sauce. After simmering, drain and cool to room temperature on a wire rack as directed. Then transfer the cooled gnocchi to a baking sheet that has been lined with kitchen parchment and misted with cooking spray; cover with plastic wrap and refrigerate for up to 24 hours. Remove the gnocchi from the refrigerator about 1 hour before you're ready to finish and serve the dish.

Kosher salt

2½ cups all-purpose flour, plus more for dusting

In a large saucepan, bring 2½ cups water to a boil over medium-high. Reduce to low and add 1½ teaspoon salt. While stirring with a silicone spatula, gradually add the flour. After all the flour has been added, cook the mixture, stirring constantly, until it forms a smooth, stiff, evenly moistened dough, about 2 minutes. Remove the pan from the heat.

Lightly dust the counter with flour, set the dough on top and lightly flour the dough; the dough will be still hot to the touch. Using a rolling pin, roll the dough about ½ inch thick (exact dimensions do not matter), then use a bench scraper to fold the dough into thirds. Repeat the process 3 or 4 more times, or until the dough is still warm to the touch but workable; add more flour as needed to prevent sticking. Using your hands, knead the dough until smooth and elastic, about 3 minutes. Cover with a kitchen towel and let rest for 15 minutes. Meanwhile, line a rimmed baking sheet with kitchen parchment. Set a wire rack in another rimmed baking sheet.

Using the bench scraper, divide the dough into 4 pieces and re-cover with the towel. Using your hands, roll one piece of dough against the counter into a rope about 18 inches long and about ¾ inch in diameter. Cut the rope into ½-inch pieces and lightly dust the pieces with flour. Dip the back of the tines of a fork into flour, then gently press into each piece to create a ridged surface. Transfer the gnocchi to the parchment-lined baking sheet; try to not allow them to touch. Shape the remaining pieces of dough in the same way.

In a large pot, bring 4 quarts water to a boil. Add 1 tablespoon salt followed by about a third of the gnocchi. Return to a boil, stirring once or twice, and cook for 2 minutes (the gnocchi will float to the surface even before they are cooked through). Using a slotted spoon and allowing excess water to fall back into the pot, transfer the gnocchi to the prepared rack; spread them out so they don't touch. The gnocchi will be very soft at this point, but will firm up as they cool. Return the water

to a boil, then cook and drain the remaining gnocchi in the same way, in two more batches.

After the final batch of gnocchi has been transferred to the rack, reserve cooking water as needed for saucing; discard the remainder. Let the gnocchi cool for at least 10 minutes or up to 1 hour to allow them to firm up.

Gnocchi in an Instant

Start to finish: 1 hour, plus cooling
Makes about 2 pounds, serving 4 to 6

These "instant" gnocchi might lack some of the earthy notes and subtle butteriness of those made with just-cooked russet potatoes, but if paired with a flavor-packed sauce, you'll be hard-pressed to notice. For make-ahead convenience, after cooking, the gnocchi can be cooled completely on the wire rack, then transferred to a baking sheet that has been lined with parchment and misted with cooking spray to prevent sticking; cover with plastic wrap and refrigerate for up to 24 hours. For longer storage, instead of refrigerating the gnocchi, freeze them until solid, about 2 hours, then transfer to a zip-close bag and freeze for up to a month. To thaw, spread the dumplings in an even layer on a lightly oiled baking sheet and let stand at room temperature until soft to the touch, about 1 hour. Heat the chilled or thawed gnocchi directly in a sauce that is already hot, tossing until warmed through.

2 cups instant potato flakes

2 cups boiling water

2 large eggs, lightly beaten

2 cups all-purpose flour, plus more for dusting

Kosher salt

Line a rimmed baking sheet with kitchen parchment. Set a wire rack in another rimmed baking sheet. Set aside. In a large bowl, stir together the potato flakes and boiling water. Let stand until cooled to room temperature. Add the eggs, flour and 1 teaspoon salt, then mix with your hands just until the ingredients form a dough. Lightly dust the counter with flour and turn the dough out onto it. Gently knead until the dough is smooth.

Using a bench scraper, divide the dough into 4 pieces and re-cover with the towel. Using your hands, roll one piece of dough against the counter into a rope about 18 inches long and about ¾ inch in diameter. Cut the rope into ½-inch pieces and lightly dust the pieces with flour. Dip the back of the tines of a fork into flour, then gently press into each piece to create a ridged surface. Transfer the gnocchi to the parchment-lined baking sheet; try to not allow them to touch. Shape the remaining pieces of dough in the same way.

In a large pot, bring 4 quarts water to a boil. Add 1 tablespoon salt followed by about a third of the gnocchi. Return to a boil, stirring once or twice, and cook for 2 minutes (the gnocchi will float to the surface even before they are cooked through). Using a slotted spoon and allowing excess water to fall back into the pot, transfer the gnocchi to the prepared rack; spread them out so they don't touch. The gnocchi will be very soft at this point, but will firm up as they cool. Return the water to a boil, then cook and drain the remaining gnocchi in the same way, in two more batches.

After the final batch of gnocchi has been transferred to the rack, reserve cooking water as needed for saucing; discard the remainder. Let the gnocchi cool for at least 10 minutes or up to 1 hour to allow them to firm up.

Homemade Orecchiette

Start to finish: 2 hours, plus resting
Makes about 1 pound uncooked pasta

Small and cup-shaped, orecchiette, meaning "little ears," come from southern Italy. The pasta traditionally is made using only semolina: a strong flour milled from durum wheat with a high gluten content. Our version calls for equal parts semolina and all-purpose flour: the latter keeps the dough soft for easy workability while the former provides the structure and elasticity required for shaping it, as well as nutty-sweet flavor. Using the instructions below, the same dough can be formed into cavatelli, a small shell pasta that resembles a tiny hot dog bun, and pici, a rustic hand-rolled spaghetti. When cooking fresh orecchiette, keep in mind it will take only about five minutes to reach al dente, which is considerably less time than store-bought dried orecchiette. The pasta is best cooked within a few hours of shaping.

1¼ cups all-purpose flour,
plus more as needed

1¼ cups semolina flour,
plus more as needed and
for dusting

Kosher salt, for cooking

To make the dough in a food processor: In a food processor, combine both flours; pulse a few times to combine. With the machine running, slowly add ¾ cup water through the feed tube. Process until the dough forms pea-sized clumps, about 25 seconds. If the dough is too sandy and dry to form clumps, pulse in more water, a few drops at a time; if the dough feels sticky, add more all-purpose flour or semolina, a sprinkle at a time.

To make the dough by hand: In a large bowl, whisk together both flours. Make a well in the center, then add ¾ cup water. Using a fork, stir in a circular motion, starting in the center and gradually moving outward to incorporate the water and flour mixture, until a shaggy dough forms. Using your hands, bring the dough together and knead, swiping along the edges of the bowl to incorporate any dry bits. If the dough resists coming together, add more water, a few drops at a time; if the dough feels sticky, add more all-purpose flour or semolina, a sprinkle at a time. The dough should be moist enough to form a cohesive mass without sticking to the sides of the bowl; it's fine if it's a little crumbly.

Lightly dust the counter with semolina and turn the dough out onto it. Knead until soft, smooth and springy, about 10 minutes. Form into a ball, cover with plastic wrap and let rest at room temperature for at least 20 minutes or for up to 1 hour. Alternatively, wrap tightly in plastic wrap and refrigerate up to 2 days; if refrigerated, let the dough stand at room temperature for 1 hour before proceeding.

Lightly dust 2 rimmed baking sheets with semolina. Unwrap the dough and cut it into quarters. Set 3 pieces aside and cover lightly with plastic wrap. Using your palms, roll the remaining piece into a log. Lightly dust the counter with semolina, then roll the log to form a rope about ½ inch in diameter; if the rope's length becomes difficult to manage, cut it in half, then roll the pieces separately.

Homemade Cavatelli

Follow the recipe to make the dough and portion the first piece into ¼-inch pieces. Dust a gnocchi board with semolina or have ready a dinner fork. Holding the board or fork, with the backside of the tines facing up, at an angle, press a piece of dough into the board or fork tines with the side of your thumb and swipe downward; the dough will curl, creating a U shape with ridges on the outer side. Transfer to a prepared baking sheet and repeat with remaining dough.

01

02

03

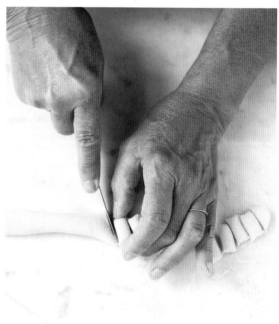

04

Cut the rope into ¼-inch pieces and lightly dust with semolina. On an unfloured area of the counter, set 1 piece cut side up. Press the flat of your thumb into the center of the piece and, while applying light pressure, smear or drag the dough against the counter with slight twisting action; the dough may curl a bit around your thumb. The finished shape should resemble a shallow cup that is thinner at the center and thicker at the perimeter. Set the orecchiette on a prepared baking sheet. Shape the remaining dough pieces in the same way; try to keep the orecchiette separated on the baking sheet to avoid sticking. Repeat with remaining dough. If not cooking right away, let stand uncovered at room temperature up to 4 hours.

To cook the orecchiette, follow the directions in the pasta recipe you are making, or in a large pot, bring 4 quarts water to a boil. Add 1 tablespoon salt and the orecchiette, then cook, stirring occasionally, until al dente. Reserve some of the cooking water if directed in your recipe, then drain the pasta.

05

Hand-Rolled Thick Spaghetti (Pici)

Follow the recipe to make and rest the dough, then cut it in half. Flatten both pieces into disks; cover one lightly with plastic wrap. Dust the counter with semolina and set the second disk on top. Using a rolling pin dusted with semolina, roll the disk to an even ⅛-inch thickness. Using a chef's knife and a decisive cutting motion (do not use a sawing action), slice the dough into ¼-inch thick strips. Lightly dust the counter with semolina, then using your fingertips, gently roll the dough back and forth against the counter into long, thin noodles about ⅛ inch in thickness. Transfer to a prepared baking sheet, keeping the noodles separate to avoid sticking. Repeat with remaining dough.

06

Cool Noodles

Cambodian-Style Rice Noodle Salad with Shrimp, Cucumber and Herbs

Start to finish: 20 minutes
Servings: 4 to 6

This noodle salad is a version of one that we tasted in Cambodia. Vegetables, herbs and chopped peanuts add tons of color and texture to tender rice vermicelli noodles. Cambodia is famous for its Kampot pepper—here we use a generous measure of ground black pepper plus a fresh chili to add multilayered spiciness to the savory-sweet dressing. We like the salad best with a combination of cilantro, mint and basil, but it's still delicious made with only one herb. And if you like, omit the shrimp or substitute 2 cups shredded cooked chicken.

8 ounces rice vermicelli

1 English cucumber, halved lengthwise, seeded and thinly sliced into half moons

1 medium shallot, halved and thinly sliced

Kosher salt and ground black pepper

1 cup roasted peanuts, finely chopped

6 tablespoons lime juice

1 Fresno or Thai chili, stemmed, seeded and minced

3 tablespoons fish sauce

2 tablespoons packed brown sugar

1 pound cooked shrimp, roughly chopped

1½ cups chopped fresh cilantro, mint and/or basil

Bring a large pot of water to a boil. Add the noodles and cook until tender, 2 to 3 minutes. Drain in a colander, then rinse under running cold water, tossing, until fully cooled. Drain again. Use kitchen shears to snip the noodles in several places to cut them into shorter lengths. Transfer to a large bowl; set aside.

In the colander, toss the cucumber and shallot with 1 teaspoon salt. Let drain in the sink for about 5 minutes. In a small bowl, stir together the peanuts, lime juice, chili, fish sauce, sugar and 2 teaspoons pepper. Add the cucumber-shallot mixture, shrimp and cilantro to the bowl with the noodles. Add the dressing and toss well.

Pearl Couscous and Zucchini Salad with Tomato Vinaigrette

Start to finish: 35 minutes
Servings: 4

This hearty salad was inspired by a recipe in the book "Shaya" by New Orleans chef Alon Shaya. Tomato paste browned with garlic in olive oil forms a rich base for the dressing. Thinly sliced fresh zucchini adds subtle crunch while tomatoes offer succulence, and salty, tangy feta ties everything together. Serve as a light vegetarian main course or as a side to grilled or roasted meats.

¼ cup extra-virgin olive oil

4 medium garlic cloves, thinly sliced

⅓ cup tomato paste

1½ teaspoons grated lemon zest, plus 2 tablespoons lemon juice and lemon wedges, to serve

Kosher salt and ground black pepper

1 cup pearl couscous

1 pint grape or cherry tomatoes, quartered

2 medium zucchini, quartered lengthwise and thinly sliced on the diagonal

1 cup lightly packed fresh mint, torn if large, divided

4 ounces feta cheese, crumbled (1 cup), divided

In an 8-inch skillet over medium, heat the oil and garlic until just sizzling. Add the tomato paste and cook, stirring with a silicone spatula, until slightly darkened, 5 to 7 minutes. Scrape the mixture into a large bowl. Whisk in the lemon zest and juice, ¾ teaspoon salt and 1 teaspoon pepper. Set aside.

In a large saucepan, bring 2 quarts water to a boil. Add 1 tablespoon salt and the couscous, then cook, stirring occasionally, until al dente, about 5 minutes. Drain and rinse until cool to the touch, then drain again.

Stir the couscous into the tomato paste mixture. Fold in the tomatoes and zucchini, followed by ¾ cup of mint and ½ cup of feta. Taste and season with salt and pepper. Transfer to a serving dish and sprinkle with the remaining mint, the remaining feta and additional pepper. Serve with lemon wedges.

Thai Pork, Glass Noodle and Herb Salad

Start to finish: 40 minutes
Servings: 4

The minced-meat salad known as larb is a traditional dish from the Isaan region in northeastern Thailand. The version we make, known as larb woon sen, features glass noodles (woon sen in Thai) that look almost translucent when cooked. You might find them labeled as bean threads, bean vermicelli or cellophane noodles. Toasted rice powder, or khao kua, is a key ingredient in larb—it contributes unique flavor, absorbs a small amount of the liquid, and brings a bit of crunch and nuttiness to the dish. The dish is finished with lots of fresh mint and cilantro.

4 ounces glass noodles (see headnote)	1 teaspoon grapeseed or other neutral oil
Boiling water, to soak the noodles	8 ounces ground pork
2 tablespoons jasmine rice	Kosher salt and ground black pepper
1 to 2 teaspoons red pepper flakes	1 cup lightly packed fresh mint
3 tablespoons fish sauce	1 cup lightly packed fresh cilantro
3 tablespoons lime juice, plus lime wedges to serve	2 scallions, thinly sliced
2 teaspoons white sugar	
1 large shallot, halved and thinly sliced	

Place the noodles in a medium heatproof bowl and add boiling water to cover. Let stand until the noodles are tender, about 15 minutes. Drain in a colander and rinse under cold water. Using kitchen shears, snip the noodles in several places to cut them into shorter lengths.

While the noodles soak, in a 10-inch skillet over medium, toast the rice, stirring often, until golden brown, 6 to 8 minutes. Transfer to a small bowl and cool for about 10 minutes.

While the rice cools, in the same skillet over medium, toast the pepper flakes, stirring, until fragrant, 30 to 60 seconds. Transfer to a large bowl, then add the fish sauce, lime juice, sugar and shallot; whisk to combine. Set the dressing aside and reserve the skillet.

Using a spice grinder or mortar and pestle, pulverize the toasted rice to a coarse powder. Return the powder to the small bowl; set aside.

In the same skillet over medium-high, heat the oil until shimmering. Add the pork and cook, breaking the meat into fine bits so there are no clumps, until no longer pink, 4 to 5 minutes. Immediately add the pork and any juices to the dressing, along with the noodles, ¼ teaspoon salt, ½ teaspoon black pepper and half of the rice powder; toss well. Let stand for 10 to 15 minutes, tossing occasionally.

Add the mint, cilantro and scallions; toss. Taste and season with salt and black pepper, then transfer to a serving dish and sprinkle with the remaining rice powder. Serve with lime wedges.

Sesame Noodles with Chicken and Scallions

Start to finish: 30 minutes
Servings: 4

For this recipe, we use non-instant dried ramen (that is, not the kind sold 10 packages for a dollar). Ramen noodles get their golden hue from an alkali—not from egg—mixed into the dough. In addition to altering the color, the alkali makes the noodles chewier, bouncier and more resilient. Dried ramen is sometimes formed into squiggly-noodled bricks (similar to instant ramen) and sometimes spaghetti-straight strands. Noodles called chuka soba or chukamen will work, too. If Italian pasta is the only type of noodle available, see How to "Ramenize" Pasta, p. 179. We like to serve these noodles with a drizzle of chili oil.

6 tablespoons sesame seeds

¼ cup grapeseed or other neutral oil

1 tablespoon toasted sesame oil

3 tablespoons soy sauce, plus more as needed

3 tablespoons unseasoned rice vinegar, plus more as needed

2 tablespoons mirin

1½ tablespoons roughly chopped fresh ginger

10 ounces non-instant dried ramen noodles (see headnote)

1½ cups shredded cooked chicken

1 bunch scallions, thinly sliced

In an 8-inch skillet over medium, toast the sesame seeds, stirring often, until fragrant and lightly browned, 3 to 4 minutes. Measure 1 tablespoon into a small bowl and set aside for garnish; add the remaining seeds to a blender and let cool for a few minutes.

To the blender, add the grapeseed oil, sesame oil, soy sauce, vinegar, mirin, ginger and 2 tablespoons water. Blend until smooth, about 20 seconds, scraping the blender jar as needed; set aside.

In a large pot, bring 2 quarts water to a boil. Add the ramen and cook, stirring occasionally, until tender (refer to the package for timing, but begin checking a few minutes earlier). Drain the noodles in a colander. Rinse under cold running water, tossing well, until fully cooled, then drain again.

Add the noodles to a large bowl. Add the chicken, half of the scallions and the sesame dressing. Toss until evenly coated. Taste and season with additional soy sauce and vinegar, if needed. Serve sprinkled with the remaining scallions and toasted sesame seeds. Offer chili oil at the table, if using.

Japanese Macaroni Salad

Start to finish: 35 minutes
Servings: 4 to 6

Like curry rice and tonkatsu, this macaroni salad is an example of yoshoku cuisine: a Western-influenced style of Japanese cooking. This salad typically is made with Kewpie—a custardy, yolk-rich Japanese mayonnaise with vinegar. To replicate Kewpie's flavor, we toss cooled macaroni in a mixture of tangy rice vinegar and American-style mayonnaise. The salad is a delicious side to grilled soy-seasoned meats and poultry. Serve it sprinkled with shichimi togarashi, a Japanese seven-spice blend, or furikake, a sesame seed and seaweed condiment.

8 ounces elbow macaroni

Kosher salt and ground black pepper

1 cup mayonnaise

3 tablespoons unseasoned rice vinegar

1 English cucumber, halved lengthwise, seeded and thinly sliced on the diagonal

1 medium carrot, peeled and shredded on the large holes of a box grater

½ medium red onion, halved and thinly sliced

6 ounces smoked deli ham, preferably ¼ to ½ inch thick, chopped (about ⅔ cup)

Shichimi togarashi or furikake, to serve (optional)

In a large saucepan, bring 2 quarts water to a boil. Add the macaroni and 1½ teaspoons salt. Cook, stirring occasionally, until fully tender. Drain in a colander and rinse under cold water, tossing well, until cool to the touch. Drain again, shaking the colander to remove as much water as possible.

While the macaroni cooks, in a large bowl, whisk together the mayonnaise, vinegar and 1 teaspoon pepper. In a medium bowl, toss the cucumber, carrot and onion with 1 teaspoon salt; let stand for at least 5 minutes or until ready to use.

Add the macaroni and ham to the mayonnaise mixture and toss to coat. Using your hands, squeeze the vegetables to remove excess liquid, then add them to the macaroni; stir until well combined. Taste and season with salt. Serve sprinkled with shichimi togarashi (if using).

Vietnamese Rice Noodle Bowls with Broiled Marinated Pork

Start to finish: 50 minutes
Servings: 4

The southern Vietnamese dish called bún thịt nướng combines bouncy, flavor-absorbing rice noodles with fresh vegetables, grilled marinated pork, herbs, peanuts and other garnishes. Individual bowls are served with a savory-sweet sauce called nước chấm on the side. Ours is a simplified version, and one that broils the pork in lieu of grilling it. To create thin, even slices of the meat, freeze the pork, uncovered, until firm to the touch but not frozen solid, about 20 minutes, then slice. Look for rice vermicelli that are round, not flat, and slender like thin spaghetti but not filament-thin. If you cannot find them in the international aisle of the grocery store, gluten-free rice-based capellini is a decent substitute.

For the sauce (nước chấm):

⅓ cup fish sauce

3½ tablespoons lime juice

¼ cup white sugar

3 medium garlic cloves, finely grated

1 or 2 serrano chilies, stemmed and minced

For the pork, noodles and garnishes:

1 tablespoon fish sauce

1 tablespoon grapeseed or other neutral oil

2 medium garlic cloves, finely grated

2 teaspoons white sugar

1¼ teaspoons Chinese five-spice powder

Kosher salt and ground black pepper

1 pound boneless pork shoulder, trimmed and sliced against the grain ⅛ to ¼ inch thick (see headnote)

14 to 16 ounces round rice vermicelli (see headnote)

½ head romaine lettuce, shredded (about 3 cups)

½ English cucumber

2 cups lightly packed torn fresh mint, cilantro or a combination

½ cup roasted peanuts, chopped

To make the sauce, in a small bowl, combine the fish sauce, lime juice, sugar and 6 tablespoons water. Stir until the sugar dissolves, then stir in the grated garlic and chilies. Cover and refrigerate up to 3 days; bring to room temperature before serving.

To prepare the pork, in a medium bowl, stir together the fish sauce, oil, garlic, sugar, five-spice, ¼ teaspoon salt and 1 teaspoon pepper. Add the pork and toss to coat. Cover and refrigerate for at least 1 hour or up to 24 hours.

Heat the broiler with a rack about 4 inches from the element. Place a wire rack in a broiler-safe rimmed baking sheet. Distribute the pork in an even layer on the rack; it's fine if the pieces do not lay perfectly flat. Broil until charred at the edges, 4 to 6 minutes. Using tongs, flip the slices and broil until well browned on the second sides, another 4 minutes.

To prepare the noodles, while the pork cooks, bring a large pot of water to a boil. Add the noodles and cook, stirring occasionally, until tender. Drain in a colander and rinse under cold running water until completely cooled, then drain again.

To assemble, divide the lettuce among 4 serving bowls, then top with noodles, dividing them evenly. Thinly slice the cucumber on the diagonal. Stack several slices and cut lengthwise into matchsticks. Repeat with the remaining slices. Divide the cucumber evenly among the bowls. Cut any large pieces of pork into bite-size strips and divide among the bowls, followed by the mint and peanuts. Serve with the sauce on the side.

Vietnamese Rice Noodle Bowls with Broiled Marinated Tofu

Drain a **14- to 16-ounce container firm tofu,** then cut the tofu into ½-inch slabs and pat dry with paper towels. Follow the recipe, substituting the tofu for the pork; the broiling technique and timing for the tofu is the same as for the pork. When assembling, cut the broiled tofu into large bite-size pieces before dividing evenly among the bowls.

Pasta with Fresh Tomatoes, Capers and Herbs

Start to finish: 25 minutes
Servings: 4 to 6

The tiny Italian island of Pantelleria off the coast of Sicily is the home of pesto pantesco, a puree of fruity olive oil, fresh tomatoes, leafy herbs, briny capers and pungent garlic. For a quick, summery dinner, we deconstructed the pesto and created a rustic no-cook sauce to toss with hot, just-drained pasta, creating a sort of pasta salad (the dish is warm, not hot, when served). Toasted almonds add crunch and pecorino cheese adds a sharpness that rounds out the flavors.

1 pound ziti or rigatoni pasta

Kosher salt and ground black pepper

½ cup extra-virgin olive oil

3 medium garlic cloves, finely grated

3 tablespoons drained capers

1 teaspoon red pepper flakes

1½ pounds ripe tomatoes, cored and chopped

1 cup lightly packed fresh mint, roughly chopped

1 cup lightly packed fresh basil, roughly chopped

½ cup sliced almonds, toasted

2 ounces pecorino Romano cheese, finely grated (1 cup)

In a large pot, bring 4 quarts water to a boil. Add the pasta and 1 tablespoon salt, then cook, stirring occasionally, until al dente. Meanwhile, in a large bowl, stir together the oil, garlic, capers, pepper flakes and ½ teaspoon each salt and black pepper. Add the tomatoes, mint and basil, then toss.

When the pasta is done, drain well. Add the pasta to the tomato-herb mixture and toss. Sprinkle with the almonds and cheese, then toss again. Taste and season with salt and black pepper.

Chilled Sesame-Soy Korean Noodles with Gochujang

Start to finish: 30 minutes
Servings: 4

Bibim guksu, which translates from the Korean as "mixed noodles," is a refreshing cold noodle dish that's a perfect meal on a hot day. The most common version is red and fiery with kimchi and gochujang (Korean fermented chili paste), but this recipe takes a milder, more soy- and sesame-centric approach to the flavoring. Somen is the Japanese name for the type of dried wheat noodle to use here; in Korean they are called somyeon. If somen is not available, soba, or Japanese buckwheat noodles, is a good alternative. If you wish to make it more substantial, top each serving with slivers of hard-cooked egg.

3 tablespoons soy sauce

2 tablespoons toasted sesame oil, plus more to serve

1½ tablespoons unseasoned rice vinegar

1½ tablespoons white sugar

1 tablespoon gochujang

1 medium garlic clove, finely grated

Kosher salt and ground black pepper

10 to 12 ounces somen noodles (see headnote)

2 cups shredded napa cabbage

1 medium carrot, peeled and shredded on the large holes of a box grater

2 scallions, thinly sliced on the diagonal

Sesame seeds, toasted, to serve

Bring a large pot of water to a boil. Meanwhile, in a large bowl, whisk together the soy sauce, sesame oil, vinegar, sugar, gochujang, garlic and ½ teaspoon each salt and pepper.

Add the noodles to the boiling water and cook, stirring often, until tender, 2 to 4 minutes. Drain in a colander, rinse under cold running water, tossing constantly, until cool to the touch, then drain again, shaking the colander to remove as much water as possible.

To the sauce mixture, add the noodles, cabbage and carrot; toss well. Taste and season with salt and pepper, then transfer to a serving bowl. Sprinkle with the scallions and sesame seeds and drizzle with additional sesame oil.

Chilled Soba with Ginger and Edamame

Start to finish: 30 minutes
Servings: 4

Chilled soba is a quintessential Japanese noodle dish, and a favorite on hot summer days. The classic version, called zaru soba, is a minimalist pairing of just noodles and a dipping sauce. Here, we include a few colorful garnishes to round out the meal, and we pour a soy-seasoned broth around the noodles instead of offering sauce on the side. Dashi, the base of this broth and a key ingredient in countless Japanese dishes, is a stock most commonly made with kombu (a type of seaweed) and katsuobushi (shavings of smoked, dried tuna). You can make your own dashi (see recipe p. 79) but store-bought instant dashi, prepared according to the package instructions, works well; look for it in the international aisle of the supermarket.

2½ cups dashi (see headnote), room temperature

4 teaspoons soy sauce

1 tablespoon mirin

1 teaspoon packed brown sugar

½ cup frozen shelled edamame

12 ounces soba noodles

1 small carrot, peeled and shredded on the large holes of a box grater

4 ounces daikon radish, peeled, finely grated and very gently squeezed to remove excess moisture (about ¼ cup; optional)

2 tablespoons finely grated fresh ginger

4 scallions, thinly sliced on the diagonal

In a medium bowl or 1-quart liquid measuring cup, combine the dashi, soy sauce, mirin and sugar; stir until the sugar dissolves. Set aside until ready to use.

Bring a large pot of water to a boil. Add the edamame and cook until tender. Using a slotted spoon, transfer to a bowl of ice water; keep the water in the pot at a boil. Let stand until the edamame are cool to the touch, then drain and set aside.

To the boiling water, add the soba and cook, stirring occasionally, until tender. Drain in a colander and rinse under cold running water, tossing constantly, until cool to the touch, then drain again, shaking the colander to remove as much water as possible.

Divide the soba evenly among 4 serving bowls. Arrange the edamame, carrot, daikon (if using), ginger and scallions on top, evenly dividing the ingredients. Pour the dashi mixture around the noodles and serve immediately.

Vietnamese Summer Rolls with Peanut Sauce

Start to finish: 1½ hours
Makes 12 rolls

Full of freshness and bright crunch, Vietnamese summer rolls make a light, refreshing meal or a crowd-pleasing appetizer. Known as gỏi cuốn, the rolls feature a filling of rice vermicelli noodles plus crisp vegetables and leafy herbs. Traditionally, both pork and shrimp are added, but to streamline, we skip the pork. Be sure to use super-thin, wiry rice vermicelli; it's sometimes labeled as maifun.

For the peanut sauce:

1 tablespoon grapeseed or other neutral oil

2 medium garlic cloves, minced

¼ teaspoon red pepper flakes

¼ cup creamy no-sugar peanut butter

3 tablespoons hoisin sauce, plus more if needed

2 tablespoons lime juice

1 tablespoon fish sauce

1 tablespoon Sriracha sauce

For the summer rolls:

24 medium-large (31/40 per pound) shrimp, peeled (tails removed) and deveined

4 to 5 ounces thin rice vermicelli noodles (see headnote)

12 soft lettuce leaves, such as Bibb, Boston or butter lettuce

1¼ cups shredded peeled carrots (2 medium), shredded peeled daikon (about 6 ounces) or a combination

1 cup lightly packed fresh mint, cilantro or a combination

Twelve 8½-inch rice paper wrappers

To make the peanut sauce, in a small saucepan over medium, combine the oil, garlic and pepper flakes; cook, stirring, until the garlic sizzles. Stir in the peanut butter and hoisin, then whisk in ½ cup water a little at a time. Bring to a simmer, then remove from the heat.

Transfer to a small bowl, then whisk in the lime juice, fish sauce and Sriracha. Taste and add more hoisin if you prefer a sweeter sauce, then cool completely. If desired, thin the sauce with up to 2 tablespoons water. (The sauce can be covered and refrigerated for up to 4 days. Bring to room temperature before serving.)

To make the summer rolls, bring a medium saucepan of water to a boil. Fill a large bowl with ice water. Add the shrimp to the boiling water, then remove the pan from the heat. Let stand until the shrimp are opaque throughout, 2 to 3 minutes.

Using a slotted spoon, transfer the shrimp to the ice water to cool; reserve the saucepan and water. Drain the shrimp and pat dry. Transfer to a cutting board and cut each one in half horizontally (head to tail); set aside. Return the water to a boil.

Add the noodles to the boiling water and cook, stirring occasionally, until tender, 3 to 4 minutes. Drain in a colander, rinse under cold running water until completely cooled, then drain again.

Mist a rimmed baking sheet with cooking spray, then line with plastic wrap and lightly mist with cooking spray. Set a wide bowl of warm water nearby, along with the noodles, lettuce, carrots, mint and shrimp.

Soak 1 rice paper wrapper in the warm water until starting to soften, about 5 seconds. Lay it flat on a cutting board or countertop. Press down on the spine of 1 lettuce leaf to flatten it, then place the leaf horizontally on the bottom third of the rice paper, tearing it to fit and leaving a 1-inch border on the bottom and sides. Top the lettuce with about ¼ cup (1 ounce) noodles, about 1 tablespoon

shredded carrots and some of the mint, distributing the ingredients evenly along the lettuce. Bring the lower part of the wrapper up over the filling and roll tightly just until the filling is enclosed and forms a cylinder. Place 4 shrimp halves, cut sides up and end to end, on the wrapper just above the cylinder. Fold in the sides of the wrapper and continue rolling to enclose the shrimp.

Set the roll on the prepared baking sheet and cover lightly with plastic wrap. Repeat with the remaining rice paper wrappers and filling ingredients. Serve right away or cover tightly with plastic wrap and refrigerate for up to 4 hours. Serve with the peanut sauce.

Cold Ramen Salad with Soy and Sesame Dressing

Start to finish: 45 minutes
Servings: 4

Vibrant and refreshing, the Japanese chilled noodle dish known as hiyashi chuka translates as "cold Chinese noodles"—chuka is the word for Chinese-style noodles as well as an alias for ramen. Essentially a composed salad, it features cold ramen with a medley of colorful toppings to be tossed into the noodles at the table, just before eating. The dish is flexible, so feel free to experiment with the toppings. Some versions are served with a richer dressing that includes sesame paste, though we opted for a lighter one made with soy sauce, rice vinegar, sesame oil, ginger and a little sugar; this imparts savory-tangy-sweet flavors to the noodles. To snip the nori use kitchen shears or scissors.

4½ tablespoons unseasoned rice vinegar

¼ cup soy sauce

1½ tablespoons plus 1 teaspoon toasted sesame oil, divided

1 tablespoon mirin

2 tablespoons white sugar

1 to 2 teaspoons finely grated fresh ginger

1½ tablespoons sesame seeds

2 large eggs, lightly beaten

½ English cucumber

10 ounces non-instant dried ramen noodles

4 ounces sliced deli ham, cut into ¼-inch strips

3 scallions, thinly sliced on a sharp diagonal

1 cup cherry or grape tomatoes, halved

0.35-ounce package roasted seaweed snacks, snipped with kitchen shears into thin strips (optional)

In a small bowl, combine the vinegar, soy sauce, 1½ tablespoons sesame oil, the mirin, sugar, ginger and 1 tablespoon water. Whisk until the sugar dissolves; set aside.

In a 10-inch nonstick skillet over medium, toast the sesame seeds, stirring often, until fragrant and lightly browned, 3 to 4 minutes. Transfer to a plate.

In the same skillet over medium, heat the remaining 1 teaspoon sesame oil until shimmering. Add the eggs and swirl the pan to distribute into a thin, even layer. Cook, without stirring, until the surface is almost dry and the bottom is lightly browned, 2 to 3 minutes. Slide the eggs onto a cutting board. Cool, then cut into 3 strips; stack the strips and slice into ¼-inch ribbons. Thinly slice the cucumber on the diagonal, then stack several slices and cut lengthwise into matchsticks. Repeat with the remaining slices.

In a large pot, bring 4 quarts water to a boil. Add the ramen and cook, stirring occasionally, until tender, then drain in a colander. Rinse under cold water, tossing well, until fully cooled, then drain again.

Divide the noodles among 4 shallow serving bowls, then arrange the eggs, ham, scallions, tomatoes and cucumber on top in separate piles, evenly dividing the ingredients. Sprinkle with sesame seeds. Stir the dressing to recombine, then drizzle about 3 tablespoons over around each portion. Mound seaweed snacks (if using) in the center of each portion. (Alternatively, to serve family style, assemble the salad on a single serving dish; toss to combine at the table, just before serving).

Toasted Orzo Salad with Roasted Pepper, Feta and Herbs

Start to finish: 45 minutes
Servings: 4 to 6

This pasta salad was inspired by the Greek feta and red pepper spread called htipiti. Toasting the orzo in olive oil until golden before simmering gives the rice-shaped pasta a rich, nutty flavor and aroma. Lemon juice brightens the flavors and balances the saltiness of the feta, while pistachios add texture and fresh dill and mint bring green, grassy notes. Freshly roasted bell pepper is preferable, but substituting 1 cup of jarred roasted red peppers works, too; just pat them dry before chopping.

1 large red bell pepper

1 tablespoon plus ¼ cup extra-virgin olive oil, divided

1 cup orzo

Kosher salt and ground black pepper

2 tablespoons lemon juice

3 ounces feta cheese, crumbled (¾ cup)

¼ cup roasted pistachios, chopped

¼ cup lightly packed fresh dill, finely chopped

¼ cup lightly packed fresh mint, thinly sliced

Heat the broiler with a rack about 6 inches from the element. Place the pepper on a broiler-safe rimmed baking sheet and broil, turning occasionally, until blackened on all sides, 14 to 16 minutes. Place in a large bowl, cover and let steam for about 20 minutes to loosen the skin. Peel the skin off the pepper and remove and discard the stem and seeds, then chop the flesh into roughly ½-inch pieces; set aside, reserving the bowl.

Meanwhile, in a large saucepan over medium, combine 1 tablespoon oil and the orzo. Cook, stirring occasionally, until the orzo is golden brown, about 5 minutes. Add 8 cups water and 1 teaspoon salt and bring to a boil. Cook over medium, stirring occasionally, until the orzo is tender. Drain in a colander, rinse with cold running water and set aside.

In the reserved bowl, whisk together the remaining ¼ cup oil, lemon juice and ¼ teaspoon salt. Add the roasted pepper, feta, pistachios, dill and mint; stir to combine. Add the orzo and stir again. Taste and season with salt and pepper. Serve immediately.

Noodle Soups

Taiwanese Beef Noodle Soup

Start to finish: 2¾ hours (45 minutes active)
Servings: 6

Niu rou mian, or beef noodle soup, is one of Taiwan's signature dishes. Chuang Pao-hua, founder of the Chung-Hua Culinary Teaching Center in Taipei, taught us how to make the hearty meal the slow, traditional way. Our much-simplified version uses fragrant star anise and Sichuan peppercorns to flavor the soup, along with toban djan, a spicy, fermented chili-bean paste. It's sold in most Asian markets, but if you can't find it, substitute with 2 tablespoons white miso mixed with 4 teaspoons Asian chili-garlic sauce and 2 teaspoons soy sauce. The soup is lightly spicy; you can add more toban djan or some ground Sichuan pepper at the table for more heat. Chinese wheat noodles of any thickness worked well, as did Japanese udon and long, thin pastas such as spaghetti.

1 tablespoon grapeseed or other neutral oil

6 garlic cloves, smashed and peeled

4-inch piece fresh ginger, peeled, cut into 6 to 8 pieces and smashed

6 scallions, whites roughly chopped, greens thinly sliced, reserved separately

3 star anise pods

1 tablespoon Sichuan peppercorns

3 tablespoons chili bean sauce (toban djan, see headnote)

2 tablespoons tomato paste

2 tablespoons packed dark brown sugar

⅓ cup soy sauce

⅓ cup sake

2 to 2½ pounds bone-in beef shanks (about 1 inch thick), trimmed

Kosher salt

1 pound baby bok choy, trimmed and cut crosswise into 1-inch pieces

8 ounces dried wheat noodles (see headnote)

In a large Dutch oven over medium, combine the oil, garlic, ginger and the white scallion parts. Cook, stirring, until sizzling, about 3 minutes. Stir in the star anise and peppercorns, then cook until fragrant, about 30 seconds. Stir in the chili-bean sauce, tomato paste, brown sugar, soy sauce, sake and 2½ quarts water. Bring to a boil over high.

Add the beef shanks and return to a simmer. Cover, reduce to low and cook, adjusting as needed to maintain a gentle simmer, until the beef is tender and beginning to fall apart, about 2 hours.

Use a slotted spoon to transfer the beef shanks to a bowl and set aside. Pour the cooking liquid through a fine-mesh strainer set over a large bowl; discard the solids. Reserve the pot. Skim off and discard the fat from the surface of the liquid, then return to the pot. When cool enough to handle, shred the meat into bite-size pieces, discarding the bones, fat and gristle. Add the meat to the pot and bring to a simmer over medium-high, then reduce to low and cover to keep warm.

In a large pot, bring 4 quarts water to a boil. Add 1 tablespoon salt and the bok choy. Cook until the stems are crisp-tender, about 3 minutes. Use a slotted spoon to transfer the bok choy to a large plate and set aside. Add the noodles to the water and cook until tender. Drain, rinse under lukewarm water, then drain again.

Divide the noodles and bok choy among serving bowls then ladle in the soup and sprinkle with scallion greens.

Soupe au Pistou

Start to finish: 35 minutes
Servings: 4

Soupe au pistou is a humble, hearty vegetable, bean and pasta soup from Provence. We learned our version from home cook Agnes Daragon. The soup takes its name from the pistou—a heady, pesto-like puree of basil, garlic, cheese and olive oil—that garnishes individual bowlfuls. For ease, we opt for canned cannellini beans as well as store-bought pesto, but feel free to use homemade. Serve the soup with hunks of crusty bread.

2 tablespoons extra-virgin olive oil, plus more to serve

1 medium yellow onion, chopped

1 pint cherry tomatoes

2 medium garlic cloves, finely chopped

1 quart low-sodium chicken broth

2 bay leaves

1 teaspoon dried thyme

Kosher salt and ground black pepper

4 ounces small pasta, such as ditalini or elbows

1 medium (about 8 ounces) zucchini, cut into ½-inch cubes

Two 15½-ounce cans cannellini beans, rinsed and drained

4 tablespoons basil pesto, divided, plus more to serve

In a large pot over medium-high, heat the oil until shimmering. Add the onion and tomatoes, then cook, stirring occasionally, until the onion begins to brown and the tomatoes begin to break down, 5 to 7 minutes.

Add the garlic and cook, stirring, until fragrant, about 45 seconds. Add the broth, bay, thyme, 1 teaspoon salt, 1 teaspoon pepper and 2 cups water, then bring to a simmer. Stir in the pasta and zucchini. Cook, uncovered and stirring occasionally, until the zucchini is almost tender, 5 to 6 minutes.

Add the beans and cook, stirring occasionally, until the pasta is al dente, the zucchini is completely tender and the beans are warmed through, 3 to 4 minutes. Remove and discard the bay. Using tongs, gently squeeze any tomatoes that are still whole so they burst.

Taste and season with salt and pepper. Ladle into bowls, then swirl 1 tablespoon pesto into each serving and drizzle with additional oil. Serve with additional pesto on the side.

Chicken Pho

Start to finish: 1 hour 40 minutes (40 minutes active)
Servings: 4

Vietnamese chicken pho, or phở gà, is a lighter noodle soup than the better-known beef pho (phở bò); it also is simpler to prepare. The key to the best flavor is the broth, of course, so we take the time to make it from scratch. After cooking, the meat is shredded, then added to individual bowls. Onion and fresh ginger are roasted in the oven to bring out their natural sweetness, and whole spices are toasted to enhance their flavor and aroma. As for the noodles, use dried rice sticks that are about ¼ inch wide. Northern-style pho typically is eaten plain, but feel free to serve the pho southern style, with fresh Thai basil, bean sprouts and sliced jalapeño along with Sriracha and hoisin.

2 medium yellow onions, unpeeled and halved

3-inch piece fresh ginger, unpeeled and halved lengthwise

4 teaspoons coriander seeds

1 tablespoon black peppercorns

3 star anise pods

3 pounds chicken drumsticks

1 bunch cilantro, roughly chopped, stems and leaves reserved separately

3 tablespoons fish sauce

2 tablespoons packed light brown sugar

Kosher salt and ground black pepper

8 to 10 ounces dried rice stick noodles

Lime wedges, to serve

Heat the oven to 425°F with a rack in the middle position. Line a rimmed baking sheet with foil. Peel and thinly slice 1 onion half crosswise. Submerge the slices in a bowl of cold water. Cover and refrigerate until needed.

Place the remaining unpeeled onion halves and ginger, cut sides down, on the baking sheet. Place the coriander seeds, peppercorns and star anise on a small piece of foil. Fold the foil up over the spices, then place on the baking sheet. Roast for 10 minutes, then remove the spice packet (it's fine if the spices are lightly smoking) and set aside. Roast the onions and ginger until the cut side of the onion halves are deeply browned and the ginger is slightly shriveled, about another 20 minutes. Cool, then peel the onions and roughly chop the ginger (no need to peel).

In a large pot over medium-high, combine the chicken, cilantro stems, fish sauce, sugar, 1 teaspoon salt, the roasted onion and ginger, the spices (removed from the packet) and 2½ quarts water. Bring to a boil, reduce to medium and simmer, uncovered, for 1 hour. Using tongs, transfer the drumsticks to a plate and set aside to cool.

Strain the broth through a mesh strainer over a large saucepan; press on the solids to extract as much liquid as possible. Discard the solids. Rinse the pot, then fill with water and bring to a boil. Heat the broth over low and cover to keep warm. When the chicken is cool enough to handle, shred the meat, discarding the skin and bones.

When the water is boiling, add the noodles and cook, stirring until just shy of tender. Drain, shaking the colander to remove as much water as possible. Divide the noodles among 4 serving bowls.

Drain the sliced onion and divide among the bowls, followed by the chicken. Bring the broth to a boil, then taste and season with salt and pepper. Ladle the broth into the bowls, then top with cilantro leaves and additional pepper. Serve with lime wedges.

Harissa-Spiced Beef and Pasta Soup

Start to finish: 1¼ hours
Servings: 4 to 6

On any given evening during the month of Ramadan, a soup similar to this graces many Libyan tables. Packed with fork-tender meat, plump orzo, warming spices and bright herbs, the comforting meal is adored nationwide—so much so that it's called "shorba," meaning, quite simply, soup, with no confusion as to which soup is being referred to. Seasoning the dish with dried mint is a must; its citrusy notes balance the harissa, a smoky North African pepper paste that brings both chili heat and complex spicing to the soup. Though optional, we love incorporating Aleppo pepper for additional layers of bright yet earthy heat.

2 tablespoons extra-virgin olive oil, plus more to serve

1 pound boneless beef short ribs, trimmed and cut into ½-inch cubes

Kosher salt and ground black pepper

2 tablespoons harissa paste

½ teaspoon ground turmeric

¼ teaspoon ground cinnamon

6-ounce can tomato paste (⅔ cup)

15½-ounce can chickpeas, rinsed and drained

¾ cup orzo pasta

1 large ripe tomato, cored and finely chopped

1 cup lightly packed fresh flat-leaf parsley, finely chopped

2 tablespoons lemon juice

1 tablespoon dried mint

1 teaspoon Aleppo pepper, plus more to serve (optional)

In a large Dutch oven over medium-high, heat the oil until shimmering. Add the beef in an even layer and season with ½ teaspoon salt and ¼ teaspoon black pepper. Cook, without stirring, until browned on the bottom, about 4 minutes. Continue to cook, stirring occasionally, until the beef is browned all over, 4 to 6 minutes.

Add the harissa, turmeric and cinnamon; cook, stirring, until fragrant, about 30 seconds. Add the tomato paste and cook, stirring, until the paste begins to brown and stick to the pot, 2 to 3 minutes. Stir in the chickpeas and 8 cups water. Bring to a simmer, uncovered, over medium-high; reduce to medium and cook, stirring occasionally, for 25 minutes.

Stir in the orzo and cook, uncovered and stirring often to prevent sticking, until the orzo and beef are tender, 15 to 20 minutes.

Off heat, stir in the tomato, parsley, lemon juice, mint and Aleppo pepper (if using). If desired, thin the soup by adding up to 1 cup hot water. Taste and season with salt and black pepper. Serve drizzled with additional oil and sprinkled with additional Aleppo pepper (if using).

Greek Orzo and Tomato Soup

Start to finish: 45 minutes
Servings: 4

In Greek, manestra refers to the rice-shaped pasta known as orzo in English and Italian, as well as to the tomato-based dish that's made with the pasta. This humble dish is often thick, almost like a risotto, and sometimes includes meat. We've turned the ingredients into a hearty vegetarian soup by simmering tomatoes, carrots, potatoes and zucchini with aromatic oregano and allspice. A sprinkling of pleasantly salty feta provides a nice contrast to the savory vegetables. Serve crusty bread alongside for dipping.

¼ cup extra-virgin olive oil, plus more to serve

1 medium yellow onion, finely chopped

4 medium garlic cloves, minced

1 teaspoon dried oregano

¼ teaspoon ground allspice

Kosher salt and ground black pepper

¼ cup tomato paste

1 medium carrot, peeled, quartered lengthwise and sliced ¼ inch thick

8 ounces Yukon Gold potatoes, peeled and cut into ½-inch cubes

14½-ounce can diced tomatoes

½ cup orzo

1 medium zucchini, quartered lengthwise and sliced ¼ inch thick

4 ounces feta cheese, crumbled (1 cup)

In a large saucepan over medium-high, heat the oil until shimmering. Add the onion, garlic, oregano, allspice and ½ teaspoon each salt and pepper. Cook, stirring occasionally, until the onion is translucent, 4 to 5 minutes. Add the tomato paste and cook, stirring, until the paste begins to brown and stick to the pot, about 1 minute.

Add the carrot, potatoes, tomatoes with juices, 1 teaspoon salt, ¼ teaspoon pepper and 6 cups water; bring to a simmer, scraping up any browned bits. Add the orzo, reduce to medium and cook, uncovered and stirring often to prevent sticking, until the orzo is barely tender, about 20 minutes. Add the zucchini and cook, uncovered and stirring often, until the orzo is fully tender and the zucchini is tender-crisp, another 5 to 10 minutes.

Off heat, taste and season with salt and pepper. Serve drizzled with additional oil and sprinkled with feta.

Chicken Noodle Soup with Turmeric and Coconut Milk

Start to finish: 1 hour 10 minutes (40 minutes active)
Servings: 4

The popular Burmese soup known as ohn no khao swe is a culinary melting pot featuring ingredients and influences from neighbors of the country now known as Myanmar, including chickpea flour, turmeric and ginger from India; coconut milk from Thailand; and noodles from China. The chickpea flour helps to thicken the soup and lends a silky texture; if you prefer to omit it, just add all of the chicken broth to the soup at once. We prefer thinnish Asian egg noodles, but feel free to swap in other types, such as flat rice noodles, thicker round rice noodles or even dried egg fettuccine or tagliatelle. If you like, offer a selection of garnishes on the side for diners to add as they please, including fresh cilantro leaves, hard-cooked eggs, crunchy wonton strips and chili-garlic sauce.

1½ pounds boneless, skinless chicken thighs, trimmed and cut into ½-inch pieces

6 medium garlic cloves, finely grated

1½ tablespoons finely grated fresh ginger

2 teaspoons ground turmeric

2 teaspoons sweet paprika

½ teaspoon cayenne pepper

Kosher salt

4 tablespoons fish sauce, divided

¼ cup plus 2 tablespoons chickpea flour (see headnote)

4 cups low-sodium chicken broth, divided

3 tablespoons grapeseed or other neutral oil

2 large yellow onions, halved and thinly sliced

14-ounce can coconut milk

1 pound fresh Asian egg noodles (see headnote)

Lime wedges, to serve

In a medium bowl, stir together the chicken, garlic, ginger, turmeric, paprika, cayenne, 1½ teaspoons salt and 1 tablespoon of the fish sauce. In a small bowl, whisk together the chickpea flour and 1 cup of the broth; set aside.

In a large Dutch oven over medium, heat the oil until shimmering. Add the onions and ½ teaspoon salt. Cook, stirring occasionally, until light golden brown, 12 to 15 minutes; reduce the heat if the onions are browning too quickly. Add the chicken and cook over medium, stirring occasionally, until opaque on the exterior, about 5 minutes.

Stir in the remaining 3 cups broth, the remaining 3 tablespoons fish sauce, the coconut milk and 3 cups water. Bring to a simmer over medium-high. Whisk the chickpea flour mixture to recombine, then whisk it into the broth mixture. Return to a simmer and cook, uncovered and stirring occasionally, until the chicken is cooked through, about 15 minutes. Off heat, taste and season with salt.

While the soup simmers, bring a large pot of water to a boil. Add the noodles and cook, stirring occasionally, until tender. Drain in a colander and rinse under cold water, shaking the colander to remove as much water as possible. Divide the noodles evenly among 4 serving bowls, then ladle the soup over the noodles. Serve with lime wedges.

Soba Noodle Soup with Chicken and Watercress

Start to finish: 35 minutes
Servings: 4

Kamo nanban soba is a classic Japanese soup that combines duck and soba noodles (kamo means duck). Inspired by the dish, we created a version that uses chicken thighs. We also added peppery watercress for vibrant color. Soba noodles, made from buckwheat flour or a blend of buckwheat and wheat flour, bring an appealing nuttiness to the soup; if you like, swap them for udon noodles, which are made from wheat flour and have a chewier texture. Umami-rich dashi forms the foundation of the delicate broth. You can make your own (see recipe p. 79), or for easy preparation, use instant dashi—just dissolve in hot water according to the package directions. Though it's optional, a sprinkling of aromatic shichimi togarashi, a Japanese seven-spice blend, lends a kick of heat and citrusy notes to the soup.

8 cups dashi
(see headnote)

¼ cup plus 3 tablespoons
soy sauce

¼ cup plus 3 tablespoons
mirin

½ teaspoon white sugar

1½ pounds boneless,
skinless chicken thighs,
trimmed and cut into
1-inch pieces

10 to 12 ounces dried soba
noodles (see headnote)

½ bunch watercress,
trimmed of tough stems,
cut into 3-inch pieces
(about 2½ cups)

3 scallions, thinly sliced

Shichimi togarashi,
to serve (optional)

In a large saucepan over medium-high, combine the dashi, soy sauce, mirin and sugar; bring to a simmer. Add the chicken and return to a simmer, then reduce to medium and simmer, uncovered and stirring occasionally, until the chicken is opaque throughout, 8 to 10 minutes.

While the soup simmers, bring a large pot of water to a boil. Add the noodles and cook, stirring occasionally, until tender. Drain in a colander, rinse under warm water and drain again, shaking the colander to remove as much water as possible. Divide the noodles evenly among 4 serving bowls.

Ladle the soup over the noodles, then top with the watercress and scallions. Serve with shichimi togarashi (if using).

Spicy Peruvian-Style Beef and Noodle Soup

Start to finish: 45 minutes
Servings: 4 to 6

This hearty, comforting dish is our take on sopa criolla, or "creole soup," a Peruvian staple with Italian roots. In addition to ground beef and capellini, the soup stars ají panca paste, a robust, red concentrate made of native Peruvian peppers. We've developed our take on the recipe using an easier-to-source alternative—similarly smoky, tangy-sweet Mexican chipotle chilies in adobo. For a more traditional flavor, just replace the chipotle chili and adobo sauce with 4 tablespoons ají panca paste. To serve, toasted bread and eggs—whether fried and placed on top or poached directly in the soup—are perfect accompaniments.

1 pound ripe tomatoes, cored and finely chopped, divided

1 large red onion, finely chopped (1½ cups), divided

2 teaspoons lime juice

Kosher salt and black pepper

3 tablespoons extra-virgin olive oil

6 medium garlic cloves, minced

1 chipotle chili in adobo sauce, minced, plus 1 tablespoon adobo sauce

3 tablespoons tomato paste

12 ounces 80 percent lean ground beef

1½ tablespoons dried oregano

4 ounces capellini

⅓ cup heavy cream or evaporated milk

In a small bowl, stir together 1 cup tomatoes, ¼ cup onion, the lime juice and ¼ teaspoon each salt and pepper. Set aside until ready to serve.

In a large pot over medium-high, heat the oil until shimmering. Add the remaining onion, garlic and ¼ teaspoon salt; cook, stirring occasionally, until beginning to brown, 3 to 4 minutes. Add the chipotle chili, adobo sauce and tomato paste; cook, stirring often, until the pastes begin to brown and stick to the pot, 1 to 2 minutes. Add the ground beef and oregano. Cook, breaking the meat into bits, until beginning to brown, 2 to 3 minutes.

Add 6 cups water and bring to a simmer. Add the pasta and 2½ teaspoons salt. Cook, stirring often, until al dente, 6 to 8 minutes. Add the remaining tomatoes and cook, stirring, until heated through, about 1 minute.

Off heat, stir in the heavy cream or evaporated milk, then taste and season with salt and pepper. Serve topped with a spoonful of the reserved salsa.

Udon Noodles in Soy Broth

Start to finish: 30 minutes
Servings: 4

With only the simplest of garnishes, classic Japanese kake udon is a great way to appreciate the chewy texture and clean, wheaty flavor of homemade udon noodles (see recipe p. 5). The broth is nothing more than a combination of smoky dashi (Japanese stock) and soy sauce with a little mirin and sugar for sweetness. Homemade dashi is best, but instant dashi prepared according to the package instructions is a solid stand-in. Look for instant dashi in the international aisle of the supermarket or in Asian grocery stores. To make this soup with dried udon, use about 10 ounces and boil the noodles until tender, then rinse and portion them as directed. If using purchased udon, you won't need to shake them to remove excess starch. Shichimi togarashi is a Japanese blend of seven spices with a fiery, citrusy kick; if you like, offer it at the table as an optional garnish.

4½ cups homemade dashi (see following recipe) or instant dashi

⅓ cup soy sauce

1½ tablespoons mirin

2 teaspoons white sugar

½ recipe (about 14 ounces) homemade udon noodles (see recipe p. 5), uncooked (see headnote)

4 scallions, thinly sliced on the diagonal

Shichimi togarashi, to serve (optional)

In a large saucepan, combine the dashi, soy sauce, mirin and sugar. Bring a large pot of water to a boil. Using your hands, add the noodles to the pot, shaking them over the baking sheet to remove excess starch. Cook, stirring often, until a noodle rinsed under cold water is tender, 15 to 17 minutes. Meanwhile, bring the dashi mixture to a simmer over medium, then remove from the heat and cover.

When the noodles are done, drain in a colander, rinse under warm water and drain again. Divide the noodles evenly among 4 serving bowls. Ladle in the hot broth and sprinkle with the scallions. If desired, serve with shichimi togarashi.

Homemade Dashi

Start to finish: 20 minutes
Makes about 4½ cups

Japanese dashi is an umami-rich stock and a building block for countless dishes. This recipe for basic dashi is based on Sonoko Sakai's kombu and bonito dashi formula in "Japanese Home Cooking."

4-inch square (about ½ ounce) kombu

3½ to 4 cups (about 1 ounce) lightly packed bonito flakes (katsuobushi)

In a medium saucepan over medium, heat the kombu and 6 cups water to just below a simmer. Remove the kombu (discard it or reserve it for another use) and bring the liquid to a boil over medium-high. Turn off the heat, add the bonito flakes (katsuobushi) and steep for about 2 minutes.

Pour the broth through a fine-mesh strainer set over a medium bowl. Discard the bonito. Use the dashi right away or cool, cover and refrigerate for up to 2 days.

Spicy Korean-Style Noodle and Seafood Soup

Start to finish: 45 minutes
Servings: 4 to 6

Korean haemul jjampong is a fiery noodle and seafood soup with Chinese origins. In our simplified version, we lean on the fermented chili paste called gochujang to lend the broth a reddish hue, depth of flavor and pleasant spice. And as a base for the soup we use basic Japanese dashi, a stock made with kombu (a type of seaweed) and shaved smoked bonito. You can make your own (see recipe p. 79) or opt for store-bought instant dashi; prepare according to package directions. If dashi is not available, two 8-ounce bottles of clam juice plus 3 cups water is a decent substitute. Dried udon is a stand-in for the fresh noodles typically used in jjampong; if you're up for it, try 12 ounces homemade Asian wheat noodles (see recipe p. 9).

2 tablespoons grapeseed or other neutral oil

12 ounces green cabbage, cut into ½-inch ribbons (about 5 cups)

1 medium yellow onion, halved and sliced

1 tablespoon finely grated fresh ginger

4 medium garlic cloves, minced

3 to 4 tablespoons gochujang

2 tablespoons fish sauce

2 pounds hardshell clams (about 1½ inches in diameter), such as Manila or littleneck, scrubbed

5 cups dashi (see headnote)

8 to 10 ounces dried udon noodles (see headnote)

1 pound skinless cod fillets, cut into 3- to 4-inch chunks

8 ounces dry sea scallops, halved if medium or quartered if large, or medium shrimp (41/50 per pound), peeled and deveined (optional)

Kosher salt and ground black pepper

4 scallions, thinly sliced

Toasted sesame oil, to serve

Bring a large pot of water to a boil. Meanwhile, in a large Dutch oven over medium-high, heat the oil until barely smoking. Add the cabbage, onion and ginger; cook, stirring occasionally, until the vegetables are softened and beginning to brown, 4 to 5 minutes. Add the garlic, gochujang and fish sauce; cook, scraping up any browned bits, until fragrant, about 1 minute. Stir in the clams and add the dashi. Cover and bring to a boil, then reduce to medium and cook, stirring occasionally, until the clams open, about 5 minutes; remove and discard any that do not open.

While the clams cook, add the noodles to the boiling water. Cook, stirring occasionally, until tender. Drain in a colander, rinse briefly under warm water and drain again. Divide the noodles among 4 serving bowls.

Season the cod and scallops (if using) with salt and pepper, then place in a layer on top of the clams; do not stir. Cover and cook without disturbing for 2 minutes. Remove the pot from the heat and let stand, covered, until the fish is opaque throughout and flaky, about 6 minutes, scattering the scallops (if using) in the pot and re-covering after 2 minutes of standing.

Ladle the soup over the noodles, evenly dividing the fish and shellfish. Sprinkle with the scallions and drizzle with sesame oil.

Yunnanese-Style Pork and Rice Noodle Soup

Start to finish: 45 minutes
Servings: 4

The Yunnan province in Southwestern China is famous for its rice noodles. One of the most popular soups, known as "small pot noodles," traditionally is served in individually sized clay pots, and diners garnish as they wish. Typically, the soup includes round rice noodles that are about the thickness of spaghetti or a little thinner. Look for Chinese noodles labeled Guilin or JiangXi or equivalently sized Vietnamese rice noodles; gluten-free rice-based spaghetti also works well. Be sure to use red miso, which is darker and saltier than white miso. Condiments really enhance the dish, so add a drizzle of chili oil and a splash of vinegar and soy sauce to taste.

12 ounces green cabbage, cut into ½-inch ribbons (about 5 cups)

Kosher salt

1 pound ground pork

6 medium garlic cloves, finely grated

1 tablespoon finely grated fresh ginger

5 tablespoons soy sauce, divided, plus more to serve

10 to 12 ounces round rice vermicelli (see headnote)

2 teaspoons plus 1 tablespoon grapeseed or other neutral oil

2 tablespoons red miso (see headnote)

2 tablespoons dry sherry or Shaoxing wine

1 bunch scallions, white parts cut to 1-inch lengths, green parts thinly sliced, reserved separately

1 quart low-sodium chicken broth

1½ teaspoons Chinese black vinegar or balsamic vinegar, plus more to serve

Chili oil, to serve

In a medium bowl, combine the cabbage and 1 teaspoon salt; using your fingers, rub the salt into the cabbage. In another medium bowl, stir together the pork, garlic, ginger, 1 tablespoon soy sauce and 2 tablespoons water. Set the cabbage and pork aside.

Bring a large pot of water to a boil. Add the noodles and cook, stirring occasionally, until tender. Drain in a colander and rinse under cold water until completely cooled, then drain again. Toss with 2 teaspoons neutral oil; set aside.

In the same pot over high, heat the remaining 1 tablespoon neutral oil until shimmering. Add the pork mixture and cook, breaking it into small pieces, until starting to brown, 5 to 6 minutes. Stir in the miso until incorporated, then stir in the remaining 4 tablespoons soy sauce, the sherry and the scallion whites. Add the broth and 2 cups water. Bring to a boil, then reduce to medium-low and simmer, uncovered and stirring occasionally, for 10 minutes.

Squeeze the liquid from the cabbage back into the bowl; discard the liquid. Add the cabbage to the pot and cook, uncovered and stirring occasionally, until tender, about 7 minutes. Add the noodles and cook, stirring, until heated through, about 1 minute.

Off heat, stir in the vinegar, then divide the soup among 4 serving bowls. Sprinkle with the scallion greens and a generous drizzle of chili oil. Serve with additional soy sauce and vinegar.

Miso Ramen

Start to finish: 35 minutes
Servings: 4

Rich, umami-packed miso ramen originates in Sapporo in northern Japan. Our much-simplified rendition may raise eyebrows among ramen purists, but we think the recipe delivers solid flavor with minimal effort. Miso supplies flavor, color and character; we prefer red (or aka) miso for its assertiveness, but milder, sweeter white (shiro) miso works, too. Dashi, an umami-rich stock and a building block in the Japanese kitchen, is essential here. You can make your own (see recipe p. 79) or use instant dashi that requires only water for dissolving or steeping. We also like to add a halved soft-cooked egg to each bowl.

8 ounces ground pork

1½ tablespoons finely grated fresh ginger

6 medium garlic cloves, finely grated

1 tablespoon soy sauce

1 tablespoon toasted sesame oil

1 tablespoon mirin

4 scallions, thinly sliced (about 1 cup), divided

½ cup red miso or white miso (see headnote)

1 quart low-sodium chicken broth

1 quart dashi (see headnote)

Kosher salt

1 pound non-instant dried ramen noodles

¾ cup frozen corn kernels, thawed and patted dry

4 thin slices salted butter (optional)

Shichimi togarashi or chili oil, to serve (optional)

In a large saucepan, combine the pork, ginger, garlic, soy sauce, sesame oil, mirin and 2 tablespoons water. Mix with your hands until well combined.

Set the pan over medium-high and cook, stirring often and breaking the meat into small pieces, until the meat is no longer pink, 2 to 3 minutes. Add ½ cup of the scallions and the miso; cook, stirring, until the ingredients are well combined and the mixture is heated through, about 1 minute. Stir in the broth and dashi, then bring to a simmer. Reduce to medium and cook, uncovered and stirring occasionally, for 15 minutes.

When the broth is nearly done, in a large pot, bring 4 quarts water to a boil. Add the ramen and cook, stirring occasionally, until tender. Drain in a colander, rinse under warm water and drain again, shaking the colander to remove as much water as possible. Divide the noodles among 4 serving bowls.

Taste the broth and season with salt. Ladle the broth over the noodles. Top each bowlful with the remaining scallions, corn and a slice of butter (if using). Serve with shichimi togarashi or chili oil (if desired).

Mexican Chicken and Fideos Soup

Start to finish: 45 minutes
Servings: 4 to 6

This comforting soup, based on Mexican sopa de pollo con fideos, consists of toasted noodles in a tomatoey broth, enhanced by tender chicken and quick-charred garlic, jalapeño and onion. In place of fideos—the short, skinny wheat-based pasta traditionally used in the dish—we substitute easier-to-find capellini or vermicelli, broken into bite-sized pieces. The noodles are lightly browned, contributing toasty flavor and depth to the broth. We top each bowl with onion and cilantro for freshness and crunch, but sliced avocado or a dollop of sour cream would be delicious, too.

1 large white onion,
¾ cut into 1-inch wedges,
¼ finely chopped, reserved separately

1 jalapeño chili, stemmed

4 medium garlic cloves, peeled

28-ounce can diced fire-roasted tomatoes

Kosher salt and ground black pepper

¼ cup grapeseed or other neutral oil

6 ounces capellini or vermicelli, broken into rough 2-inch pieces (1½ cups)

1 pound boneless, skinless chicken thighs, trimmed and cut into ¾-inch pieces

6 cups low-sodium chicken broth

1 teaspoon dried oregano, preferably Mexican oregano

1 tablespoon lime juice

¼ cup lightly packed fresh cilantro, chopped

Heat the broiler with a rack about 6 inches from the element. Place the onion wedges, jalapeño and garlic on a broiler-safe rimmed baking sheet and broil, flipping the vegetables once, until blistered and charred on both sides, about 5 minutes. Transfer to a blender with the tomatoes and juices, ½ teaspoon salt and ¼ teaspoon pepper. Blend until smooth, about 1 minute; set aside.

In a large Dutch oven over medium, heat the oil until shimmering. Add the pasta and cook, stirring, until golden brown, about 2 minutes. Add the chicken and ¼ teaspoon each salt and pepper; cook, stirring occasionally, until the chicken begins to brown, 3 to 4 minutes.

Add the tomato puree and cook, uncovered and stirring occasionally, until the mixture is thick enough that a spoon leaves a trail when drawn through it, about 4 minutes. Add the broth and oregano; bring to a boil over medium-high. Reduce to a simmer and cook, uncovered and stirring occasionally, until the noodles and chicken are tender, 10 to 15 minutes.

Off heat, stir in the lime juice. Taste and season with salt and pepper. Serve sprinkled with cilantro and the reserved onion.

Chicken and Mushroom Noodle Soup with Sauerkraut

Start to finish: 45 minutes
Servings: 6

Moldovan zama and Ukrainian zeama, sour soups from Eastern Europe, inspired this chicken noodle soup that's at once comforting and new. Rustic homemade egg noodles are an ingredient in traditional versions, but to streamline, we call for ready-to-cook fresh fettuccine. For the sour power, we stir in sauerkraut brine, and punch up the flavor by adding some sauerkraut as well. This brightens the dish, balancing the earthy vegetables and meaty chicken. Fresh dill and a dollop of sour cream finish the dish.

2 tablespoons extra-virgin olive oil

1 pound boneless, skinless chicken thighs, trimmed and cut into ½-inch pieces

Kosher salt and ground black pepper

8 ounces cremini mushrooms, trimmed and quartered

1 cup drained refrigerated sauerkraut, plus ½ cup sauerkraut brine

1 medium carrot, peeled and finely chopped

1 medium yellow onion, finely chopped

3 medium celery stalks, finely chopped, leaves reserved for garnish

2 quarts low-sodium chicken broth

8- to 9-ounce package fresh fettuccine, cut into 1-inch pieces

1 tablespoon dried tarragon (optional)

½ cup lightly packed fresh dill, chopped

Sour cream, to serve

In a large Dutch oven over medium-high, heat the oil until shimmering. Add the chicken and ¼ teaspoon each salt and pepper, then cook, without stirring, until browned on the bottom, 5 to 6 minutes. Push the chicken to one side of the pot. Add the mushrooms and cook, without stirring, until they begin to brown on the bottom and release their liquid, about 5 minutes. Add the sauerkraut and brine; cook, scraping up any browned bits, until the liquid has evaporated and the sauerkraut begins to brown, about 3 minutes.

Stir in the carrot, onion, celery and ¼ teaspoon each salt and pepper. Reduce to medium, cover and cook, stirring occasionally, until the vegetables begin to soften, about 5 minutes. Stir in the broth and re-cover. Bring to a simmer over medium-high, then again reduce to medium and cook until the chicken is opaque throughout and the vegetables are tender, about 10 minutes.

Add the pasta and tarragon (if using). Cook, uncovered and stirring often, until the noodles are al dente (refer to the package for cooking times, but begin checking for doneness a minute or two sooner than the directions indicate).

Off heat, stir in the dill, then taste and season with salt and pepper. Serve garnished with sour cream and the celery leaves.

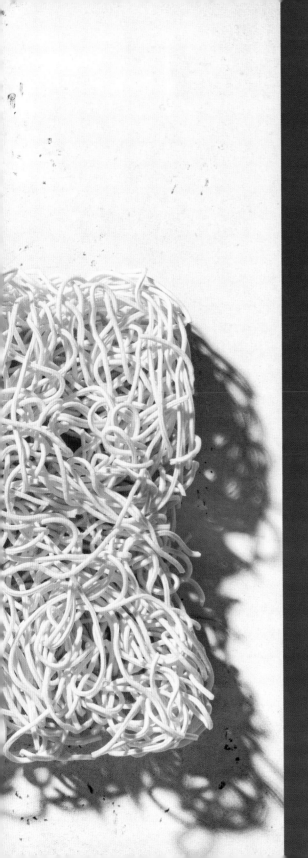

Fast & Saucy

Rigatoni with Pistachio, Ricotta and Herb Pesto

Start to finish: 25 minutes
Servings: 4 to 6

Sicily is famous for its pistachios, as well as for ricotta cheese. In this recipe, we blend the two, along with fresh basil and chives, to create a simple pesto to toss with al dente pasta. There's no need to grate the Parmesan—simply cut it into chunks and toss the pieces into the blender. The pesto is good on a wide variety of pasta shapes, but the hollow centers and surface ridges of rigatoni do a particularly good job of gripping the rich, creamy sauce.

1 pound rigatoni or other short tubular pasta

Kosher salt and ground black pepper

1⅓ cups whole-milk ricotta cheese

¾ cup raw pistachios, plus 2 tablespoons finely chopped pistachios

2 tablespoons extra-virgin olive oil, plus more to serve

2 ounces Parmesan cheese (without rind), cut into 4 or 5 pieces

½ cup lightly packed fresh basil

¼ cup roughly chopped fresh chives

In a large pot, bring 4 quarts water to boil. Stir in the pasta and 1 tablespoon salt, then cook, stirring occasionally, until al dente. Reserve 1½ cups of the cooking water, then drain the pasta and return it to the pot.

In a blender, combine the ricotta, the whole pistachios, oil, Parmesan, basil, chives, ½ teaspoon salt and ¼ teaspoon pepper. Add 1 cup of the reserved pasta water and blend until creamy, about 1 minute; the pesto should have a consistency similar to yogurt.

Pour the pesto over the pasta and stir, adding more reserved pasta water as needed so the sauce coats the noodles. Taste and season with salt and pepper. Serve drizzled with additional oil and sprinkled with the chopped pistachios.

Soba Noodles with Asparagus, Miso Butter and Egg

Start to finish: 25 minutes
Servings: 4

Japanese soba noodles, made with earthy buckwheat, find good company in grassy asparagus, umami-rich white miso, sweet butter and fiery fresh ginger. For evenly cooked asparagus, we separate the tender tips from the sturdier stalks; we toss the stalks, cut into pieces, into the noodle cooking water first, and a minute later add the tips. Asparagus that measures about ½ inch at the thickest end works best in this recipe. Most brands of soba cook in about 4 minutes. For noodles that need longer (check the package instructions), adjust the timing for adding the asparagus. Runny-yolk fried eggs are the perfect topping to round out the meal. While the soba cooks, heat the skillet, then fry the eggs while tossing the noodles with the miso butter.

1 pound medium asparagus (see headnote), trimmed

⅓ cup white miso

4 tablespoons salted butter, room temperature

1½ tablespoons finely grated fresh ginger

12 ounces soba noodles

3 scallions, finely chopped, plus thinly sliced scallions to serve

4 fried eggs

Shichimi togarashi, to serve (optional)

Lemon wedges, to serve

Bring a large pot of water to a boil. Meanwhile, snap or cut off the tender tips of the asparagus; set aside. Slice the stalks on the diagonal into ½-inch pieces; set aside separately. In a large bowl, combine the miso, butter and ginger, then mash and stir until well combined.

To the boiling water, add the noodles and cook, stirring, for 1 minute. Add the asparagus stalks and cook for 1 minute more. Add the tips, then cook, stirring occasionally, until the noodles are tender and all of the asparagus is tender-crisp, about 2 minutes. Reserve ½ cup cooking water, then drain.

Add the soba-asparagus mixture and the chopped scallions to the miso-butter mixture. Using tongs, toss until the butter is melted and the noodles are well coated; add reserved cooking water as needed so the mixture is lightly creamy.

Divide the noodles evenly among 4 serving bowls and top each with a fried egg. Sprinkle with sliced scallions and shichimi togarashi (if using) and serve with lemon wedges.

Spaghetti with Parsley Pesto

Start to finish: 25 minutes
Servings: 4 to 6

"Spaghetti with parsley pesto" is the literal translation, from the Italian, of spaghetti al pesto di prezzemolo, and it does not sufficiently convey the deliciousness of this dish. The recipe is an adaptation of one taught to us by chef Antonio Cioffi at La Vecchia Cantina, in Ravello near the Amalfi Coast. Cioffi uses neither nuts nor Parmesan in his incredibly savory parsley pesto. Rather, its umami richness and full, complex flavor came from colatura di alici, an Italian fermented anchovy condiment akin to Southeast Asian fish sauce. Colatura di alici is saltier, less pungent and smoother in taste than fish sauce. It does require a trip to an Italian specialty store; we found a single oil-packed anchovy fillet, rinsed and patted dry, to be a good substitute. We also adopted Cioffi's technique of quickly blanching the parsley before pureeing it; this step is key for creating a luxurious, silky-smooth pesto with an emerald green hue.

Kosher salt and ground black pepper

1 large bunch flat-leaf parsley (about 4 ounces), trimmed of bottom 1 inch

1 small garlic clove, smashed and peeled

2½ teaspoons colatura di alici (see headnote) or 1 oil-packed anchovy fillet, rinsed and patted dry

¾ cup extra-virgin olive oil, plus more to serve

1 pound spaghetti

4 teaspoons grated lemon zest, plus 4 teaspoons lemon juice, plus more grated zest to serve

In a large pot, bring 4 quarts water to a boil. Fill a medium bowl with ice water and set it near the stovetop. To the boiling water, add 1 tablespoon salt and the parsley; cook, stirring, until just wilted, about 15 seconds. Using a slotted spoon or mesh sieve, immediately scoop out the parsley and transfer it to the ice bath. Let stand, stirring once or twice, until fully chilled, about 2 minutes. Reduce the heat under the pot to medium.

Remove the parsley from the ice bath and squeeze with your hands until mostly dry. Roughly chop the parsley, then add it to a blender along with the garlic, colatura de alici or anchovy, and the oil. Puree on high, scraping the blender jar as needed, until the mixture is smooth and thick, 1 to 2 minutes. If the parsley doesn't fully break down, while the blender is running, drizzle in cold water 1 teaspoon at a time as needed until the pesto is smooth.

Return the water to a boil over medium-high. Add the pasta and cook, stirring occasionally, until al dente. Reserve about ¾ cup of the cooking water, then drain the pasta and return it to the pot. Add the pesto and ½ cup of the reserved pasta water; cook over medium, vigorously tossing and stirring, until the pesto clings to the spaghetti, about 2 minutes. Stir in the lemon zest and juice and toss in more reserved pasta water 1 tablespoon at a time as needed so the spaghetti is well sauced. Remove from the heat, then taste and season with salt and pepper. Serve drizzled with additional oil and sprinkled with additional lemon zest.

Miso-Walnut Soba with Bok Choy

Start to finish: 20 minutes
Servings: 4

Nutty, wholesome Japanese buckwheat noodles and bok choy are sauced with a puree of toasted walnuts and miso that delivers a double hit of umami. The starchy water that results from cooking soba is called soba yu; we use a little of it to help the sauce blend smoothly and cling to the noodles. You can use either sweeter, milder white miso, or saltier, earthier red miso—or even a blend if you happen to have both. To add a little citrusy heat and hints of sesame, offer shichimi togarashi, a Japanese spice blend, at the table for sprinkling to taste.

10 ounces dried soba noodles

1 pound baby bok choy, trimmed and thinly sliced crosswise

⅓ cup walnuts, toasted, plus chopped toasted walnuts, to serve

3 tablespoons white miso or red miso

2 tablespoons grapeseed or other neutral oil

2 medium garlic cloves, smashed and peeled

Kosher salt and ground black pepper

Lemon wedges, to serve

Bring a large pot of water to a boil. Add the soba and cook, stirring occasionally, until al dente. Reserve ¾ cup cooking water, then add the bok choy to the pot and cook until the soba is tender and the bok choy is crisp-tender, about 1 minute. Drain in a colander, rinse and drain again; return to the pot.

In a blender, combine 3 tablespoons of the reserved cooking water, the walnuts, miso, oil and garlic; puree until smooth. Add the walnut-miso mixture to the soba mixture, then toss, adding more reserved water as needed to the noodles are lightly sauce. Taste and season with salt and pepper. Serve sprinkled with chopped toasted walnuts and with lemon wedges.

Garlic and Black Pepper Noodles with Shrimp and Chives

Start to finish: 30 minutes
Servings: 4

The popular, deliciously buttery, umami-packed garlic noodles served at the An family's Vietnamese restaurants in Northern and Southern California inspired this quick-cooking recipe. Lots of black pepper lends an undercurrent of spiciness and piney notes and plump, briny-sweet shrimp turn the noodles into a main. We call for non-instant dried ramen, lo mein or other wheat-based noodles with a thickness similar to spaghetti. Small shrimp, 51/60 per pound, work best here as they integrate nicely with the noodles. Fresh chives or scallion greens add a pop of color and freshness, balancing the richness of the dish.

10 ounces dried non-instant ramen or other round Asian wheat noodles (see headnote)

6 tablespoons salted butter, cut into 1-tablespoon pieces, divided

8 medium garlic cloves, minced

2 tablespoons oyster sauce

1½ tablespoons fish sauce

12 ounces small (51/60 per pound) shrimp, peeled (tails removed) and deveined

½ cup finely chopped fresh chives or thinly sliced scallion greens

2 teaspoons coarsely ground black pepper, plus more to serve

In a Dutch oven over high, bring 4 quarts water to a boil. Add the noodles, then cook, stirring occasionally, until tender. Reserve 1 cup of the cooking water, then drain in a colander. Rinse under cold running water, then drain again; set aside.

In the same Dutch oven over medium, melt 4 tablespoons butter. Add the garlic and cook, stirring often, until fragrant, about 2 minutes. Add the oyster sauce, fish sauce and ¾ cup of the reserved cooking water; bring to a simmer. Add the shrimp and cook, stirring occasionally, until they just begin to turn pink, about 3 minutes.

Add the noodles, the remaining 2 tablespoons butter, half of the chives and all of the black pepper. Cook, stirring and tossing, until the sauce coats the noodles and the shrimp are opaque throughout, about 2 minutes; add more cooking water 1 tablespoon at a time as needed if the mixture looks dry. Serve sprinkled with the remaining chives and additional black pepper.

Pasta with Spicy Tomato and Pancetta Sauce

Start to finish: 30 minutes
Servings: 4 to 6

Zuppa forte, also known as zuppa di soffritto, is an old-school Neapolitan dish made by slow-cooking meats with garlic and other aromatics, along with tomatoes and preserved chilies, until reduced and concentrated. The rich, thick, spicy paste-like mixture can be spread on crusty bread, though it's more commonly diluted and used as soup base or pasta sauce. During a visit to Naples we especially loved the wonderfully balanced, intensely flavorful version we tasted at La Cantinetta, a tiny eatery/grocery store/wine shop where octogenarian Maria Notaro does the cooking. Zuppa forte traditionally was made with odds and ends of meats, including offal, but the Neapolitan cooks we consulted said pancetta would be a reasonable stand-in. The preserved chilies were the most difficult ingredient to approximate. We landed on Korean gochujang, which may seem out of place, but the thick, fermented paste delivers a similar complex spiciness along with welcome notes of umami. If you can source Calabrian chili paste, which is spicy, tangy and salty, it, too, is great.

14½-ounce can whole peeled tomatoes

2 tablespoons gochujang (see headnote) or 1 tablespoon Calabrian chili paste

Kosher salt and ground black pepper

¼ cup extra-virgin olive oil

4 ounces pancetta, chopped

4 medium garlic cloves, minced

4 bay leaves

2 tablespoons tomato paste

1 rosemary sprig

1 pound penne, ziti or rigatoni pasta

½ cup lightly packed fresh basil, torn

Whole-milk ricotta cheese, to serve

In a large pot, bring 4 quarts water to a boil. In a blender, puree the tomatoes with juices and gochujang until smooth, 30 to 60 seconds; set aside.

While the water heats, in a 12-inch skillet, combine the oil, pancetta, garlic, bay leaves, tomato paste, rosemary and ½ teaspoon pepper. Cook over medium, stirring often, until the pancetta has rendered some of its fat and the tomato paste darkens and begins to stick to the pan, 6 to 8 minutes. Add the pureed tomato mixture and bring to a simmer, scraping up any browned bits. Simmer, uncovered and stirring often, until very thick and the fat separates, about 10 minutes.

Meanwhile, when the water reaches a boil, add 1 tablespoon salt and the pasta; cook, stirring occasionally, until just shy of al dente. Reserve about 1½ cups of the cooking water, then drain the pasta and return it to the pot. (If the sauce is done ahead of the pasta, remove the skillet from the heat.)

Scrape the sauce into the pot with the pasta and add ¾ cup of the reserved cooking water. Cook over medium, stirring and tossing often, until the sauce clings and the pasta is al dente, 2 to 4 minutes; add more reserved pasta water as needed to loosen the noodles if the mixture is very dry and sticky.

Off heat, remove and discard the bay and rosemary. Taste and season with salt and pepper, then stir in the basil. Serve topped with dollops of ricotta.

Hoisin-Ginger Noodles

Start to finish: 20 minutes
Servings: 4 to 6

A satisfying, flavor-filled noodle dinner doesn't come together more easily and quickly than this. Hoisin provides salty-sweet umami in the no-cook sauce, ginger provides fresh, peppery punch, and chili-garlic sauce (or Sriracha) adds balancing heat along with allium notes. We use udon, a type of thick, chewy Japanese wheat noodle for this; dried lo mein works well, too. Even linguine works, if that's what you have.

12 ounces dried udon noodles or dried lo mein (see headnote)

¼ cup plus 2 tablespoons hoisin sauce

¼ cup chili-garlic sauce or Sriracha sauce

2 tablespoons toasted sesame oil

2 tablespoons soy sauce

1 tablespoon finely grated fresh ginger

3 scallions, thinly sliced

Chopped roasted salted peanuts, to serve

In a large pot, bring 4 quarts water to a boil. Add the noodles and cook, stirring occasionally, until tender. Meanwhile, in a medium bowl, whisk together the hoisin, chili-garlic sauce, sesame oil, soy sauce and ginger.

When the noodles are done, drain well in a colander, then return them to the pot. Add the hoisin mixture and toss until evenly coated. Serve sprinkled with the scallions and peanuts.

Peruvian Spinach Pesto Pasta

Start to finish: 45 minutes
Servings: 4 to 6

The origin of Peruvian pesto with pasta, or tallarines verdes ("green noodles" translated from the Spanish), dates to the 19th century, when a wave of Italian immigrants settled in Peru. Many came from Genoa—the birthplace of pesto Genovese—and they adapted the recipe to the available ingredients. A shocking amount of spinach replaces the basil, and crumbled queso fresco supplements (and sometimes entirely replaces) salty Parmesan cheese. Two types of alliums—onion and garlic—are blended into the pesto, then a quick simmer in the same pot used to boil the pasta softens their fiery edge. Another difference from Italian pesto is the addition of dairy, commonly evaporated milk, though we prefer the cleaner, sweeter flavor of heavy cream.

1 pound linguine

Kosher salt and ground black pepper

1 medium yellow onion, roughly chopped

½ cup extra-virgin olive oil

4 medium garlic cloves, smashed and peeled

1-pound container baby spinach

⅓ cup heavy cream

3 ounces Parmesan cheese, grated (about 1½ cups)

4 ounces queso fresco, crumbled (about 1 cup)

Lime wedges, to serve

In a large Dutch oven, bring 4 quarts water to a boil. Stir in the pasta and 1 tablespoon salt, then cook, stirring occasionally, until just shy of al dente. Reserve 1½ cups of the cooking water, then drain; reserve the pot.

Meanwhile, in a food processor, combine the onion, oil, garlic, ½ teaspoon salt, 1 teaspoon pepper and ¼ cup water. Add about a third of the spinach and process until smooth, about 30 seconds. Add the remaining spinach in 2 batches, processing until smooth after each.

Transfer the spinach puree to the now-empty pot. Bring to a boil over medium-high and cook, stirring occasionally, until the mixture begins to thicken, 3 to 5 minutes. Add the reserved pasta water and return to a simmer, then add the pasta and toss to coat. Cook, stirring occasionally, until the pasta is al dente and the mixture is no longer watery, 3 to 5 minutes. Stir in the heavy cream.

Off heat, stir in the Parmesan, then taste and season with salt and pepper. Serve sprinkled with the queso fresco and with lime wedges on the side.

Fettuccine with Corn, Tomatoes and Bacon

Start to finish: 35 minutes
Servings: 4 to 6

Sweet, buttery, salty and smoky are the defining flavors of this summery pasta dish that can be made year-round thanks to frozen corn. Supermarket cherry (or grape) tomatoes are dependably good no matter the season, but briefly simmering them on the stovetop brings out their sweetness and renders them juicy and succulent. We boil the fettuccine until it's not quite al dente, then finish cooking the pasta in the sauce so it absorbs flavors. Though delicious as is, we also like to garnish this pasta with chopped fresh basil or finely grated Parmesan cheese (or both).

12 ounces fettuccine or pappardelle pasta

Kosher salt and ground black pepper

4 ounces bacon, chopped

½ medium yellow onion, finely chopped

4 medium garlic cloves, minced

1½ cups frozen corn kernels, thawed

1 pint cherry or grape tomatoes, halved

2 tablespoons salted butter, cut into 2 pieces

2 teaspoons balsamic vinegar, preferably white balsamic

In a large pot, bring 4 quarts water to a boil. Add the pasta and 1 tablespoon salt, then cook, stirring occasionally, until just shy of al dente. Reserve 1 cup of the cooking water, then drain and set aside.

Meanwhile, in a large Dutch oven over medium-high, cook the bacon, stirring occasionally, until brown and crisp, 3 to 5 minutes. Using a slotted spoon, transfer the bacon to a paper towel–lined plate; set aside. Pour off and discard all but 1 tablespoon of the fat in the pot.

Return the Dutch oven to medium and add the onion and garlic; cook, stirring often, until lightly browned, 5 to 8 minutes. Stir in the corn, tomatoes and ¼ teaspoon pepper. Cover and cook, stirring once or twice, until the tomatoes have softened and released their juices, about 4 minutes.

Add the pasta and ½ cup of the reserved cooking water, then cook, stirring and tossing, until the pasta is al dente and lightly sauced, 3 to 5 minutes; add more cooking water 1 tablespoon at a time as needed if the mixture looks dry. Off heat, stir in the butter, vinegar and bacon until the butter is melted. Taste and season with salt and pepper.

Chinese Chili and Scallion Noodles

Start to finish: 25 minutes
Servings: 4

Fuchsia Dunlop's game-changing "midnight noodles" is a fresh spin on a Chinese staple. The simple sauce comes together in the time it takes the noodles to cook. Our version swaps out some of the hard-to-find Chinese ingredients and creates a simple chili oil that can be adjusted to taste. We cooked scallion whites in the hot oil to soften their bite and used the milder green parts to add brightness at the end. While we preferred udon noodles, chewy Chinese wheat noodles such as lo mein were fine substitutes. Even spaghetti worked in a pinch. These noodles also are great topped with fried eggs.

12 ounces dried udon noodles, lo mein or spaghetti

⅓ cup soy sauce

3 tablespoons unseasoned rice wine vinegar

3 tablespoons packed dark brown sugar

1 tablespoon toasted sesame oil

¼ cup grapeseed or other neutral oil

5 teaspoons sesame seeds

1¼ teaspoons red pepper flakes

2 bunches scallions, thinly sliced on the diagonal, white and green parts reserved separately

In a large pot, bring 4 quarts water to a boil. Add the noodles and cook, stirring occasionally, until tender. Meanwhile, in a large bowl, combine the soy sauce, vinegar, sugar and sesame oil; whisk until the sugar dissolves.

In a 10-inch nonstick skillet over medium, heat the grapeseed oil, sesame seeds and pepper flakes; cook, stirring, until the pepper flakes are fragrant and the sesame seeds begin to brown, 3 to 5 minutes. Remove from the heat and stir in the scallion whites, then scrape the mixture into the bowl with the soy mixture.

Add the cooked noodles to the sauce and toss to combine. Add about three-fourths of the scallion greens and toss again. Divide the noodles evenly among 4 individual bowls and sprinkle each with a portion of the remaining scallion greens.

Pasta with Fennel, Green Olive and Pistachio Pesto

Start to finish: 35 minutes
Servings: 4 to 6

With green olives and Parmesan cheese, this pesto is especially rich in umami, and the pistachios balance the saltiness with their gentle sweetness. It's not only for pasta, though—it also is delicious spread onto sandwiches or served as a relish with roasted vegetables or chicken. If you like, make the pesto ahead; it will keep in an airtight container in the refrigerator for up to two days.

1 pound medium-short pasta, such as penne, ziti or rigatoni

Kosher salt and ground black pepper

½ cup raw pistachios

2 ounces (without rind) Parmesan cheese, cut into rough 1-inch pieces, plus finely grated Parmesan to serve

½ cup pitted green olives

½ cup lightly packed fresh flat-leaf parsley

½ cup extra-virgin olive oil

1 medium garlic clove, smashed and peeled

1 teaspoon fennel seeds, toasted

In a large pot, bring 4 quarts water to a boil. Stir in the pasta and 1 tablespoon salt, then cook, stirring occasionally, until al dente. Reserve about ½ cup of the cooking water, then drain in a colander and return to the pot.

While the pasta cooks, in a food processor, combine the pistachios, Parmesan and ½ teaspoon each salt and pepper. Process until the mixture resembles coarse sand, 10 to 20 seconds. Add the olives, parsley, oil, garlic and fennel seeds; process, scraping the bowl as needed, until almost completely smooth, about another 20 seconds.

Add the pesto to the pasta in the pot along with 3 tablespoons of the reserved pasta water, then toss; add more reserved pasta water as needed so the pesto coats the noodles. Taste and season with salt and pepper. Serve sprinkled with grated Parmesan.

Pasta with Lemon and Parmesan

Start to finish: 20 minutes
Servings: 4 to 6

This simple dish may have few ingredients, but it boasts bold, bright flavors. Many versions include cream, but we preferred to use a little butter and some of the starchy spaghetti-cooking water; this gives the pasta a saucy consistency and light creaminess that doesn't mute the freshness of the lemon. Feel free to switch out linguine for the spaghetti and adjust the lemon zest and juice to your taste.

1 pound spaghetti

Kosher salt and ground black pepper

5 tablespoons salted butter, cut into 1-tablespoon pieces, divided

8 medium garlic cloves, minced

¾ to 1 teaspoon red pepper flakes

1 cup dry white wine

½ cup finely chopped fresh flat-leaf parsley or basil

2 tablespoons grated lemon zest, plus 3 tablespoons lemon juice

Finely grated Parmesan cheese, to serve

In a large pot, bring 3 quarts water to a boil. Stir in the pasta and 1 tablespoon salt; cook until just shy of al dente. Reserve 2 cups of the cooking water, then drain and set aside.

Meanwhile, in a 12-inch skillet over medium, melt 3 tablespoons butter. Add the garlic and cook, stirring, until fragrant, about 30 seconds. Add the pepper flakes and cook, stirring, until the garlic begins to turn golden, about 1 minute. Add the wine and simmer until reduced to about ½ cup, about 5 minutes.

Stir in 1½ cups of the reserved pasta water and bring to a simmer over medium-high. Add the pasta and cook, stirring and tossing, until most of the liquid has been absorbed, 2 to 3 minutes.

Off heat, add the remaining 2 tablespoons butter, ¾ teaspoon black pepper, the parsley and the lemon juice and zest. Toss until the butter is melted. Taste and season with salt and, if needed, adjust the consistency by adding additional pasta water a few tablespoons at a time. Transfer to a serving bowl and serve sprinkled with Parmesan.

Shrimp with Orzo, Tomatoes and Feta

Start to finish: 35 minutes
Servings: 4

Shrimp with feta, or garides saganaki, is a Greek classic. Adding orzo pasta and spinach to the combo, as we do here, yields a superb meal-in-one. Credit for the idea goes to chef Michael Psilakis and a recipe from his book "How to Cook a Lamb." Sear the shrimp and start the tomato sauce while the pasta water heats and the orzo cooks. We stir the spinach and feta into the orzo immediately after draining—the heat from the pasta melts the feta and gently wilts the greens. The orzo-spinach-feta mixture is fine to wait until the shrimp and sauce are finished and ready for tossing.

1½ cups orzo pasta

Kosher salt and ground black pepper

5-ounce container baby spinach

4 ounces feta cheese, crumbled (1 cup)

1 pound extra-large (21/25 per pound) shrimp, peeled (tails removed), deveined and patted dry

¼ cup extra-virgin olive oil, plus more to serve

1 medium yellow onion, chopped

3 medium garlic cloves, thinly sliced

1 tablespoon chopped fresh oregano

½ teaspoon red pepper flakes

28-ounce can whole peeled tomatoes, crushed by hand

In a large saucepan, bring 2 quarts water to a boil. Stir in the orzo and 1½ teaspoons salt, then cook, stirring occasionally, until al dente. Reserve about ½ cup of the cooking water, then drain and return the orzo to the pan. Stir in the spinach and about three-quarters of the feta; set aside uncovered.

While heating the water and cooking the pasta, season the shrimp with salt and black pepper. In a 12-inch skillet over medium-high, heat the oil until shimmering. Add the shrimp in an even layer and cook without stirring until lightly browned on the bottoms, about 2 minutes. Using a slotted spoon, transfer the shrimp to a bowl, leaving the oil in the pan; set aside.

Return the skillet to medium-high. Add the onion and ¼ teaspoon salt, then cook, stirring occasionally, until beginning to brown, about 5 minutes. Add the garlic, oregano and pepper flakes; cook, stirring, until fragrant, about 1 minute. Add the tomatoes with juices and bring to a simmer. Cover, reduce to medium-low and cook, stirring occasionally, for about 5 minutes.

Remove the skillet from the heat. Stir the shrimp and accumulated juices into the sauce, re-cover and let stand until the shrimp are opaque throughout, 3 to 5 minutes.

Pour the sauce over the orzo-spinach mixture in the saucepan. Stir to combine, adding reserved pasta water as needed if the mixture looks dry. Taste and season with salt and black pepper. Transfer to a serving bowl, then sprinkle with the remaining feta and drizzle with additional oil.

Chinese Hot Oil Noodles with Bok Choy

Start to finish: 30 minutes
Servings: 4

This recipe is our version of northern China's you po mian, a simple, flavor-packed noodle dish known for coming together in a flash. Cooked noodles and lightly blanched greens are topped with soy sauce, vinegar and aromatics like garlic, scallions and cilantro. The finishing touch is a few tablespoons of sizzling oil poured over the top. Flat, moderately wide noodles are ideal. Our hand-cut wheat noodles, sliced into ¼- to ½-inch wide ribbons, work perfectly, though dried udon, fettuccine or pappardelle are great, too. Malty, subtly sweet and a touch smoky, Chinese black vinegar is worth seeking out; if not available, balsamic vinegar makes a solid replacement. Make sure to use heat-proof bowls that can withstand the temperature of smoking-hot oil.

¼ cup soy sauce

1 tablespoon Chinese black vinegar or balsamic vinegar

12 ounces baby bok choy, trimmed and separated into individual leaves

12 ounces dried flat wheat noodles or 1 recipe hand-cut wheat noodles (see recipe p. 9; see headnote)

¼ cup lightly packed fresh cilantro, chopped

2 scallions, thinly sliced

¾ to 1 teaspoon red pepper flakes

4 medium garlic cloves, finely grated, divided

½ cup grapeseed or other neutral oil

Kosher salt

In a small bowl, stir together the soy sauce and vinegar; set aside. Bring a large pot of water to a boil. Add the bok choy and cook, stirring occasionally, until the stems are tender-crisp, 2 to 3 minutes. Using a slotted spoon, transfer the bok choy to a colander; keep the water at a boil. Shake the colander to remove excess water, then divide the bok choy among 4 heatproof individual serving bowls.

To the boiling water, add the noodles and cook, stirring occasionally, until just shy of tender. Drain, shaking the colander to remove as much water as possible. If using hand-cut noodles or dried udon, rinse under cold water and drain again. Divide the noodles among the bowls.

Divide the soy-vinegar mixture among the serving bowls, pouring a generous tablespoon over each. Toss the contents of each bowl to combine. Top each with the cilantro, scallions, pepper flakes and garlic; do not stir.

In a small saucepan over medium-high, heat the oil until barely smoking. Working quickly, pour 2 tablespoons oil over each bowl; you should hear a sizzle as the oil "sears" the aromatics. Toss, then serve immediately, with salt on the side for sprinkling to taste.

Linguine with Artichokes, Lemon and Pancetta

Start to finish: 30 minutes
Servings: 4 to 6

The sauce for this pasta is made by blitzing artichokes in a blender. For ease, we use canned artichokes instead of fresh, but we first brown them in a mixture of olive oil and rendered pancetta fat to build flavor in the sauce. The crisp bits of pancetta lend texture and saltiness, lemon adds brightness and balance, and a generous amount of Parmesan ties all the elements together.

1 pound linguine or fettuccine

Kosher salt and ground black pepper

1 tablespoon extra-virgin olive oil, plus more to serve

4 ounces pancetta, chopped

14-ounce can artichoke hearts, drained, patted dry and quartered if whole

1 tablespoon grated lemon zest, plus 3 tablespoons lemon juice

2 ounces Parmesan cheese, finely grated (1 cup), plus more to serve

½ cup finely chopped fresh flat-leaf parsley, chives or basil

In a large pot, bring 4 quarts water to a boil. Stir in the pasta and 1 tablespoon salt, then cook, stirring occasionally, until al dente. Reserve about 2 cups of the cooking water, then drain.

In the same pot over medium, heat the oil until shimmering. Add the pancetta and cook, stirring, until crisp, 3 to 4 minutes. Using a slotted spoon, transfer to a small plate; set aside. Add the artichokes to the pot and cook, stirring, until beginning to brown at the edges, 3 to 4 minutes. Remove the pot from the heat. Transfer half the artichokes to a small bowl; add the remainder to a blender. Reserve the pot.

To the artichokes in the blender, add ½ cup cooking water, the lemon juice and ¼ teaspoon each salt and pepper; puree until smooth. In the same pot over medium, bring 1 cup of the remaining cooking water to a simmer, scraping up any browned bits. Add the artichoke puree, the pasta, lemon zest, pancetta, Parmesan and parsley. Cook, tossing to combine, just until the noodles are heated through, 1 to 2 minutes; add more reserved water as needed to make a silky sauce. Taste and season with salt and pepper. Transfer to a serving bowl and top with the reserved artichokes, along with additional oil and Parmesan.

Gnocchi with Pancetta and Garlic

Start to finish: 30 minutes
Servings: 4 to 6

Gnocchi, the pillowy Italian dumplings, take well to a host of sauces. Here, we serve them simply, tossed with pancetta, garlic, Parmesan and red pepper flakes for a little heat, a combination inspired by a recipe we learned from Antonio Cioffi, chef at La Vecchia Cantina in Naples. This dish is equally delicious made with homemade potato gnocchi (see recipe p. 22), "instant" gnocchi made with potato flakes (see recipe p. 29) or gnocchi di farina (see recipe p. 26); to streamline prep, feel free to use store-bought gnocchi instead. Whatever type you use, follow the instructions for cooking your gnocchi first, as they are simply reheated in a skillet with a handful of ingredients for a few minutes before serving.

2 pounds gnocchi, homemade or store-bought (see headnote)

4 ounces pancetta, finely chopped

3 tablespoons extra-virgin olive oil, divided

6 medium garlic cloves, thinly sliced

¼ to ½ teaspoon red pepper flakes

2 tablespoons lemon juice

¼ cup finely chopped fresh flat-leaf parsley or basil

1 ounce Parmesan cheese, finely grated (½ cup)

Cook and drain the gnocchi according to your recipe or the package instructions, reserving about 1½ cups of the cooking water; set aside.

In a 12-inch nonstick skillet over medium, cook the pancetta, stirring often, until browned and crisped, 5 to 7 minutes. Using a slotted spoon, transfer to a small bowl; set aside. Pour off and discard all but 1 tablespoon of the fat from the pan.

Return the skillet to medium and add 1 tablespoon of the oil and the garlic. Cook, stirring often, until the garlic is light golden brown, about 2 minutes. Using the slotted spoon, transfer to the bowl with the pancetta.

Return the skillet to medium and add the gnocchi, pepper flakes and ½ cup of the reserved cooking water. Cook, stirring and tossing often, until the gnocchi are heated through, 3 to 5 minutes; add up to ½ cup more reserved water as needed to form a silky sauce. Add the pancetta and garlic; cook, stirring, until heated through, about 1 minute.

Off heat, stir in the remaining 2 tablespoons oil, the lemon juice and parsley. Taste and season with salt and black pepper. Serve sprinkled with the Parmesan.

Pasta with Cauliflower, Lemon and Pistachios

Start to finish: 30 minutes
Servings: 4

We drew on the flavors of bagna cauda—the sauce-like dip from Italy's Piedmont region—and paired the bold flavors of garlic and anchovies with pasta and cauliflower, then brightened up the mix with lemon zest and juice. The anchovies melt away, leaving behind a salty-savory tang, while butter and some of the pasta cooking water help create a quick sauce. Toasted pistachios add crunch; lemon juice and zest brighten the dish. Campanelle is a frilly, trumpet-shaped pasta that catches both cauliflower and sauce; other short pasta shapes, such as farfalle and cavatappi, also work well.

12 ounces campanelle, farfalle or cavatappi pasta

Kosher salt and ground black pepper

5 tablespoons extra-virgin olive oil, divided

⅓ cup pistachios, roughly chopped

2½-pound head cauliflower head, cored and cut into 1-inch florets

8 medium garlic cloves, minced

2 tablespoons minced oil-packed anchovy fillets, plus 2 tablespoons anchovy oil

2 teaspoons minced fresh rosemary

½ teaspoon red pepper flakes

4 tablespoons salted butter, cut into 1-tablespoon pieces, divided

1 tablespoon grated lemon zest, plus 2 tablespoons lemon juice

¾ cup lightly packed fresh flat-leaf parsley, roughly chopped

In a large pot, bring 4 quarts water to a boil. Stir in the pasta and 1 tablespoon salt, then cook, stirring occasionally, until just shy of al dente. Reserve 1 cup of the cooking water, then drain. Meanwhile, in a 12-inch skillet over medium-high, heat 1 tablespoon oil until shimmering. Add the pistachios and toast, stirring often, until fragrant and bright green, 30 to 45 seconds; transfer to a small bowl and set aside.

In the same skillet over medium, heat 2 tablespoons of the remaining oil until shimmering. Add half of the cauliflower and ¼ teaspoon each salt and black pepper. Cook, stirring occasionally, until lightly browned, about 5 minutes; transfer to a medium bowl. Repeat with the remaining 2 tablespoons oil, the remaining cauliflower and ¼ teaspoon each salt and black pepper; leave the second batch of cauliflower in the pan.

Return the first batch of cauliflower to the pan. Stir in the garlic, anchovies and oil, rosemary, pepper flakes and 2 tablespoons butter. Cook, stirring often, until the anchovies have disintegrated, 4 to 5 minutes. Add the pasta cooking water and bring to a boil over medium-high. Add the pasta and remaining 2 tablespoons butter, then cook, tossing, until the sauce has thickened and coats the pasta, about 1 minute.

Off heat, stir in the lemon juice and all but about 1 tablespoon of the pistachios. Taste and season with salt and black pepper. Serve sprinkled with the remaining pistachios, the parsley and lemon zest.

Spaghetti with Anchovies, Pine Nuts and Raisins

Start to finish: 30 minutes
Servings: 4

This pasta dish features the classic Sicilian flavor combination of savory, sweet and sour. Our version was inspired by a recipe from Vecchia Trattoria da Totò run by Guiseppe and Piera di Noto in Palermo. Toasted breadcrumbs, sprinkled on just before serving, provide pleasant crispness. We preferred fluffy panko bread-crumbs over regular powder-fine breadcrumbs, but crushing or chopping the panko before toasting ensured better blending with the pasta. Crush the panko in a zip-close plastic bag with a meat pounder or rolling pin, or simply chop it with a chef's knife on a cutting board.

12 ounces spaghetti

Kosher salt and ground black pepper

6 tablespoons extra-virgin olive oil, divided, plus more to serve

⅓ cup panko breadcrumbs, finely crushed or chopped (see headnote)

¼ cup pine nuts, finely chopped

3 tablespoons golden raisins, finely chopped

10 oil-packed anchovy fillets, patted dry

8 medium garlic cloves, finely chopped

2 tablespoons white wine vinegar

½ cup lightly packed fresh flat-leaf parsley, chopped

In a large pot, bring 4 quarts water to a boil. Add the spaghetti and 1 tablespoon salt, then cook, stirring occasionally, until just shy of al dente. Reserve about 1½ cups of the cooking water, then drain the pasta.

While the pasta cooks, in a 12-inch skillet over medium, combine 2 tablespoons oil and the panko. Cook, stirring often, until golden brown, 3 to 5 minutes. Transfer to a small bowl and set aside; wipe out the skillet.

Set the skillet over medium-high and add the remaining 4 tablespoons oil, the pine nuts, raisins, anchovies and garlic. Cook, stirring, until the anchovies have broken up and the garlic is golden brown, about 2 minutes. Stir in the vinegar and cook until syrupy, 30 to 60 seconds. Add 1 cup of the reserved pasta water and ¼ teaspoon each salt and pepper and bring to a simmer.

Add the pasta, reduce to medium, and cook, occasionally tossing to combine, until the pasta is al dente and has absorbed most of the moisture but is still a little saucy, about 2 minutes. Remove from the heat. If the pasta is dry, add more cooking water, 1 tablespoon at a time. Stir in the parsley, then taste and season with salt and pepper. Transfer to a serving bowl. Sprinkle with the panko and top with additional oil and pepper.

Farfalle with Zucchini, Pecorino and Basil

Start to finish: 35 minutes
Servings: 4 to 6

Our inspiration for this dish comes from pasta alla nerano, an Italian classic from the Amalfi Coast that features spaghetti in a velvety zucchini sauce with semi-firm Provolone del Monaco cheese. We pair farfalle with bite-sized pan-fried zucchini, all bolstered with butter for richness and pecorino Romano for savoriness. Summer squash can easily become soft and textureless, so it's important to avoid crowding the pan and fry it in two batches. To further facilitate even cooking, we slice the squash into quarter-moons, allowing the pieces to develop a uniformly golden brown hue, which builds flavor.

1 pound farfalle

Kosher salt and ground black pepper

3 tablespoons extra-virgin olive oil, divided

2 medium garlic cloves, smashed and peeled

2 medium (1 pound total) zucchini or yellow summer squash, quartered lengthwise and sliced crosswise ¼ inch thick

4 tablespoons salted butter

½ teaspoon red pepper flakes

2½ ounces pecorino Romano cheese, finely grated (1¼ cups)

1 cup lightly packed fresh basil, torn

½ cup raw unsalted shelled pistachios, finely chopped

In a large pot, bring 3 quarts water to a boil. Add the pasta and 2 teaspoons salt, then cook, stirring occasionally, until the pasta is just shy of al dente. Reserve 1½ cups of the cooking water, then drain and set aside; reserve the pot.

Meanwhile, in a 12-inch nonstick skillet over medium, combine 2 tablespoons oil and the garlic. Cook, stirring occasionally, until the garlic is golden brown, about 2 minutes. Remove and discard the garlic. Increase to medium-high and heat the oil until shimmering. Add half the zucchini and a pinch of salt; cook, stirring occasionally, until golden brown all over, about 5 minutes. Transfer to a small bowl. Using the remaining 1 tablespoon oil cook the remaining zucchini in the same way. Transfer to the bowl and set aside.

In the large pot over medium, combine the butter, pepper flakes and ¼ teaspoon salt; cook, stirring, until the butter melts. Add the pasta and reserved cooking water; cook, stirring to combine, until the pasta is al dente and lightly sauced, 2 to 3 minutes.

Off heat, add the cheese, stirring until melted and creamy. Add about two-thirds of the basil, the pistachios and the zucchini; toss to combine. Taste and season with salt and black pepper. Serve sprinkled with the remaining basil.

Turkish-Style Noodles
with Butter, Walnuts and Feta

Start to finish: 30 minutes
Servings: 4

This recipe is inspired by cevizli eriște, a Turkish pasta dish with toasted walnuts, ample butter and briny, semi-firm cheese. Eriște are short, thin egg noodles, typically made in the late summer or early fall, then dried in the sun. We've replaced them with easier-to-find fresh fettuccine, cut into bite-sized pieces. You can also use 12 ounces of dried egg noodles.

16 to 18 ounces fresh fettuccine, cut into 2-inch pieces

Kosher salt and ground black pepper

¾ cup walnuts, finely chopped

4 tablespoons salted butter

1½ teaspoons Aleppo pepper or ½ teaspoon smoked paprika plus ½ teaspoon red pepper flakes

1 teaspoon dried mint (optional)

1 teaspoon grated lemon zest, plus ¼ cup lemon juice

4 ounces feta cheese, crumbled (1 cup)

½ cup lightly packed fresh flat-leaf parsley, chopped

In a large pot, bring 4 quarts water to a boil. Add the pasta and 1 tablespoon salt, then cook, stirring often, until al dente. Reserve 1 cup of the cooking water, then drain.

Meanwhile, in a 12-inch skillet over medium, toast the walnuts, stirring often, until fragrant and lightly browned, about 4 minutes. Transfer to a small bowl; set aside.

To the skillet still over medium, add the butter and cook, stirring occasionally, until melted, about 1 minute. Add the Aleppo pepper, mint (if using) and ¼ teaspoon salt; cook, stirring, until fragrant, about 30 seconds. Add the lemon zest and juice, pasta and reserved cooking water; toss to combine. Cook, stirring occasionally, until the sauce is slightly reduced and begins to cling to the pasta, about 3 minutes. Off heat, stir in the toasted walnuts, feta and parsley, then taste and season with salt and black pepper.

Orecchiette with Sardinian Sausage Ragù

Start to finish: 35 minutes
Servings: 4 to 6

Saffron gives this simple Sardinian ragù lots of character. The spice's unique, vaguely floral, slightly minerally flavor pairs beautifully with the sausage, tomatoes and salty pecorino, but since saffron is a somewhat rarified ingredient, we've kept it optional. Even without, the dish is delicious. Our favorite pasta for this recipe is orecchiette, a coin-sized, saucer-shaped noodle that does an excellent job of catching the bits of sausage; store-bought is great but homemade (see recipe p. 30) makes the dish extra-special. Small shells and campanelle work well, too.

¼ cup extra-virgin olive oil

4 medium garlic cloves, chopped

½ cup dry white wine

¼ teaspoon saffron (optional)

14½-ounce can tomato puree (1½ cups)

1 pound sweet or hot Italian sausage, casings removed, broken into ½-inch or smaller pieces

Kosher salt

1 pound orecchiette pasta (see headnote)

1 ounce pecorino Romano cheese, finely grated (½ cup), plus more to serve

½ cup roughly chopped basil, plus more to serve

In a 12-inch skillet over medium, combine the oil and garlic. Cook, stirring, until the garlic is golden brown, 4 to 6 minutes. Add the wine and saffron (if using), then cook, stirring occasionally, until reduced by about half, 6 to 8 minutes. Stir in the tomato puree, sausage and ½ teaspoon salt. Bring to a simmer, cover and reduce to medium-low. Cook, stirring once or twice, until the pieces of sausage are no longer pink at the center, 5 to 7 minutes.

Meanwhile, in a large pot, bring 2 quarts water to a boil. Add 1½ teaspoons salt and the pasta and cook, stirring occasionally, until al dente. Reserve about ½ cup of the cooking water, then drain the pasta and return to the pot.

Transfer the sausage mixture to the pot with the pasta, then stir in the cheese and 2 tablespoons of reserved pasta water. If the sauce is too thick, stir in additional pasta water 1 tablespoon at a time until the desired consistency is reached. Taste and season with salt, then stir in the basil. Serve sprinkled with additional basil and cheese.

Italian
Classics

Skillet Cacio e Pepe

Start to finish: 20 minutes
Servings: 4

The name of this classic Roman pasta dish translates as "cheese and pepper." We developed an unusual technique of cooking the pasta in a 12-inch skillet with a minimal amount of water into which a small amount of all-purpose flour has been whisked. The starchy cooking water becomes the base for making a cheesy sauce that won't break and has a silky and creamy, but not heavy, consistency. We found it best to avoid high-end spaghetti, the type with a rough, floury appearance, as the pasta tends to release a large amount of starch during cooking, making the sauce gluey and too thick. Widely available brands such as De Cecco and Barilla work well. It's important to use true pecorino Romano cheese purchased in a chunk and to grate it finely with a rasp-style grater or grind it finely in a food processor. Cacio e pepe is at its best hot, so we recommend serving in warmed bowls to slow the rate at which the pasta cools as it's eaten.

If grating the pecorino by hand, grate it finely using a wand-style grater. If using a food processor, cut the cheese into rough ½-inch pieces and process until finely ground, 30 to 45 seconds. Transfer to a bowl and set aside.

In a 12-inch skillet, combine 5 cups water, the flour and ½ teaspoon salt; whisk until no lumps of flour remain. Bring to a boil over high, stirring occasionally. Add the pasta and cook, uncovered, stirring often and pushing the noodles into the water to keep them submerged, until the spaghetti is al dente and about ½ cup of starchy liquid remains, 10 to 12 minutes.

Remove the pan from the heat and let the pasta cool, tossing with tongs once or twice, for 1 minute. With the pan still off heat, gradually add the cheese while tossing. Once all the cheese has been added, continue tossing until fully melted. Add the oil and pepper; toss to combine. If the mixture is dry, add hot water 1 tablespoon at a time until the pasta is lightly sauced. Serve in warmed bowls sprinkled with additional pepper and cheese.

5 ounces (without rind) pecorino Romano cheese, plus finely grated cheese to serve

2 teaspoons all-purpose flour

Kosher salt

12 ounces spaghetti

3 tablespoons extra-virgin olive oil

2 teaspoons coarsely ground black pepper, plus more to serve

Hot water, if needed

Rigatoni Carbonara with Peas

Start to finish: 30 minutes
Servings: 4 to 6

A favorite Roman pasta dish, carbonara comes together easily with ingredients you likely already have in the kitchen. In place of guanciale, the type of cured pork traditionally used, we swap in smoky-sweet bacon. We also add green peas for freshness and bright color; feel free to omit them if you wish—the results will still be delicious. After draining the pasta, immediately add it to the egg and cheese mixture, then toss constantly for about a minute to coat the noodles and prevent the eggs from curdling. The pasta's residual heat will lightly cook the eggs, creating a rich, velvety coating.

4 ounces bacon, chopped

2 medium garlic cloves, smashed and peeled

1 large egg, plus 2 large egg yolks

2 ounces Parmesan cheese, pecorino Romano cheese or a combination, finely grated (1 cup), plus more to serve

Kosher salt and ground black pepper

1 pound rigatoni or ziti

1 cup frozen peas, thawed

In a 10-inch skillet over medium-high, cook the bacon, stirring occasionally, until crisp, 4 to 5 minutes. Off heat, add the garlic and stir to coat with the rendered fat; set the pan aside.

In a large bowl, whisk together the whole egg and yolks, half the Parmesan and ½ teaspoon pepper; set aside.

In a large pot, bring 3 quarts water to a boil. Add the pasta and 2 teaspoons salt, then cook, stirring occasionally, until al dente. Reserve ½ cup of the cooking water, then stir the peas into the pot with the pasta and drain. Immediately pour the pasta and peas into the bowl with the egg mixture. Toss until the pasta is lightly sauced, about 1 minute; add the reserved cooking water 1 tablespoon at a time as needed if the mixture looks dry.

Set the skillet with the bacon over medium-high and cook, stirring, until the fat starts to sizzle and the bacon is heated through, 30 to 60 seconds. Off heat, remove and discard the garlic. Pour the bacon and rendered fat over the pasta, add the remaining Parmesan and toss well. Taste and season with salt and pepper. Serve sprinkled with additional cheese.

Spaghetti with Garlic, Olive Oil and Chilies

Start to finish: 30 minutes
Servings: 4

This classic Roman dish, called pasta aglio, olio e peperoncino, requires few ingredients but packs big flavor. In our version, fresh Fresno chilies add vibrant color, a subtle fruitiness and chili heat that balances the garlic. If you're a fan of spice, you can leave the seeds in one of the Fresnos, or add a pinch or two of red pepper flakes to the oil along with the chilies and garlic. Boiling the spaghetti for only 5 minutes in a relatively small amount of water leaves the pasta only partly cooked and the water extra-starchy; we reserve some of the water to finish cooking the spaghetti in the same skillet in which we've made a garlic-and-chili infused oil.

⅓ cup extra-virgin olive oil

3 Fresno chilies, seeded, halved and thinly sliced crosswise

8 medium garlic cloves, smashed and peeled

12 ounces spaghetti

Kosher salt

½ ounce Parmesan or pecorino Romano cheese, finely grated (¼ cup), plus more to serve

¼ cup roughly chopped fresh flat-leaf parsley

In a 12-inch skillet over medium, combine the oil, chilies and garlic. Cook, stirring occasionally, until the garlic is golden brown, about 5 minutes. Remove from the heat, then transfer only the garlic to a small bowl. Use a fork to mash it to a coarse paste; set aside. Let the oil cool slightly while you cook the pasta.

In a large pot, bring 2 quarts water to a boil. Stir in 1½ teaspoons salt and the pasta; cook for 5 minutes. Reserve about 2¼ cups of the cooking water, then drain the pasta.

Add 2 cups of the reserved cooking water and the pasta to the skillet. Bring to a vigorous simmer over medium-high and cook, stirring occasionally, until the pasta is al dente and most of the liquid has been absorbed, 3 to 5 minutes.

Off heat, add the cheese, ½ teaspoon salt and the smashed garlic. Toss, adding cooking water 1 tablespoon at a time as needed so the pasta is lightly sauced, not dry. Transfer to a serving bowl, then sprinkle with the parsley. Serve with additional grated cheese.

Fettuccine Alfredo

Start to finish: 30 minutes
Servings: 4 to 6

Made the Italian way, fettuccine Alfredo bears little resemblance to the cream-based pasta dish that's popular in the U.S. We scoured Italy for the best versions, and our favorite was prepared by home cook Francesca Guccione in Castelnuovo di Porto, just outside Rome. Rich, luxurious and elegant but neither heavy nor cloying, Guccione's fettuccine Alfredo consists of only fresh pasta, Parmigiano Reggiano cheese, butter and salt. The secret lies in using high-quality ingredients and combining them in just the right way, and in just the right volumes. Of utmost importance is the cheese. Purchase a hefty chunk of true Parmigiano Reggiano—not the pre-shredded stuff—trim off the rind, cut 6 ounces into rough ½-inch pieces and whir them in a food processor until very finely ground. High-fat butter also is key. At the grocery store, some types of high-fat butter are labeled "European-style"; Plugrá and Kerrygold are two widely available brands.

8 tablespoons salted European-style butter (see headnote), sliced about ½ inch thick

6 ounces Parmigiano Reggiano cheese (without rind), cut into rough ½-inch chunks

16 to 18 ounces fresh fettuccine, homemade (see recipe p. 15) or store-bought

Kosher salt

Line a large bowl with the butter slices, placing them in a single layer along the bottom and up the sides of the bowl; let stand at room temperature until the butter is softened.

Meanwhile, in a food processor, process the cheese until very finely ground, about 40 seconds; transfer to a medium bowl (you should have about 1½ cups).

In a large pot, bring 2 quarts water to a boil. Add the pasta and 1½ teaspoons salt, then cook, stirring often, until the pasta is al dente. Remove the pot from the heat. Using tongs, transfer the pasta from the pot, with ample water clinging to it, to the butter-lined bowl. Using the tongs, quickly stir and toss the pasta, incorporating the butter, until the butter is fully melted. Add ½ cup pasta water and toss until the water has been absorbed.

Add 1 cup of the cheese, tossing, ⅓ cup at a time, tossing and adding the next addition only after the previous one has been incorporated. Next, toss in ½ to 1 cup more pasta water, adding about ¼ cup at a time, until the sauce clings to the pasta and only a small amount pools at the bottom of the bowl.

Let stand for 2 minutes to allow the sauce to thicken slightly. If needed, toss in additional pasta water a little at a time until the sauce once again clings to the pasta and only a small amount pools at the bottom of the bowl. Taste and season with salt. Divide among warmed serving bowls and serve immediately with the remaining cheese on the side for sprinkling at the table.

Lasagna Bolognese

Start to finish: 1 hour 20 minutes (30 minutes active), plus cooling
Servings: 8 to 10

Lasagna Bolognese is a delicious marriage of rich, meaty ragù, creamy besciamella (the Italian version of French béchamel sauce) and supple, tender pasta. Our take on the Italian classic was inspired by a version we tasted at Osteria Broccaindosso in Bologna. We liked Barilla oven-ready lasagna noodles, preferring them even over fresh sheet pasta. Both the ragù and the besciamella should be warm for lasagna assembly; if made ahead, the ragù reheats well in a large saucepan over medium. A serrated knife is best for cutting the lasagna for serving.

6 tablespoons salted butter, cut into 6 pieces

¼ cup all-purpose flour

1 quart half-and-half

3 bay leaves

½ teaspoon red pepper flakes

Kosher salt and ground black pepper

3 ounces Parmesan cheese, finely grated (1½ cups), plus more to serve

6 large fresh basil leaves

12 no-boil 6½-by-3½-inch lasagna noodles (see headnote)

1 tablespoon extra-virgin olive oil

6 cups ragù Bolognese (see recipe p. 146), warmed

In a large saucepan over medium, melt the butter. Whisk in the flour, then cook, whisking constantly, for 2 minutes. While whisking, gradually add the half-and-half and bring to a simmer. Add the bay and pepper flakes, then reduce to low. Cook, whisking often, until the sauce thickens, reduces slightly and no longer tastes of raw starch, 10 to 15 minutes.

Off heat, whisk in the Parmesan and basil. Cool for 5 minutes, then set a fine-mesh strainer over a medium bowl, pour the sauce into the strainer and press on the solids with a silicone spatula; discard the solids. Taste and season with salt and pepper. Cover to keep warm.

Heat the oven to 350°F with a rack in the middle position. Place the noodles in a 9-by-13-inch baking dish, then add hot water (about 140°F) to cover, along with the oil and 1½ teaspoons salt; swish the noodles around to dissolve the salt. Let stand for 10 minutes, moving the noodles around halfway through to ensure they do not stick together.

Remove the noodles from the water and arrange in a single layer on a kitchen towel; pat dry with paper towels. Wipe out the baking dish. Distribute 2 cups ragù evenly in the baking dish, then place 3 noodles in a single layer on top. Spread ¼ cup besciamella onto each noodle, all the way to the edges. Pour 1 cup ragù on top and spread evenly. Repeat the layering 3 more times, using the remaining noodles, besciamella and ragù, then cover the baking dish tightly with foil.

Bake until the edges of the lasagna are bubbling, 45 minutes to 1 hour. Transfer to a wire rack, uncover and cool for about 30 minutes. Cut into pieces and serve sprinkled with Parmesan.

Tagliatelle alla Bolognese

Start to finish: 3¼ hours (40 minutes active)
Servings: 4

Ragù Bolognese is luxuriously rich in both flavor and texture, the result of hours of slow, gentle simmering. Alberto Bettini, chef at the Michelin-starred Amerigo restaurant outside Bologna, taught us how to make the Italian classic. The key is to process chunks of beef, pork and pancetta in a food processor rather than start with store-bought ground meat. And to give the ragù rich, velvety body, we add a bit of gelatin. The classic pasta pairing is tagliatelle, which typically is made with eggs so the noodles have a richer flavor and a delicate texture. Fresh tagliatelle, store-bought or homemade (see recipe p. 15), is excellent here, but dried is fine, too. This recipe yields 8 cups of ragù—more than you will need for four servings of pasta. The remainder is just enough to make lasagna Bolognese (see recipe p. 144); it can be refrigerated for up to three days or frozen with plastic wrap pressed directly against the surface for up to one month.

4 tablespoons salted butter

3 tablespoons extra-virgin olive oil, plus more to serve

1 large yellow onion, cut into rough 1-inch pieces

1 medium celery stalk, cut into rough 1-inch pieces

1 medium carrot, peeled and cut into rough 1-inch pieces

Two 28-ounce cans whole tomatoes

1½ pounds boneless beef short ribs, cut into rough 1-inch chunks

1 pound boneless pork shoulder, cut into rough 1-inch chunks

8-ounce piece pancetta, cut into rough 1-inch chunks

¼ cup tomato paste

½ cup dry white wine

2 cups low-sodium beef broth

4 bay leaves

½ teaspoon red pepper flakes

2 tablespoons unflavored powdered gelatin

Kosher salt and ground black pepper

8.8-ounce package dried tagliatelle

Finely grated Parmesan cheese, to serve

In a large Dutch oven, combine the butter and oil. In a food processor, pulse the onion, celery and carrot until roughly chopped, about 5 pulses. Transfer to the Dutch oven. One can at a time, add the tomatoes with juices to the food processor and puree until smooth; transfer to a medium bowl. Add half the beef to the food processor and pulse until coarsely ground, 5 to 10 pulses, then transfer to another medium bowl; repeat with the remaining beef. Repeat with the pork, in batches, adding it to the beef. Finally, process the pancetta to a coarse paste, about 30 seconds; add to the other meats.

Set the pot over medium-high and cook, stirring occasionally, until the vegetables are lightly browned, about 5 minutes. Stir in the tomato paste and cook, stirring, until the paste begins to brown, about 5 minutes. Add the wine and cook, scraping up any browned bits, until the pot is almost dry, about 1 minute. Stir in the ground meats, then stir in the broth, tomatoes, bay and pepper flakes. Bring to a simmer, then partially cover, reduce to medium-low and cook, stirring occasionally,

until the meat is tender, the sauce is thick and the volume has reduced to about 8 cups, 2½ to 3 hours. Remove the pot from the heat.

Pour ¼ cup water into a small bowl and sprinkle the gelatin evenly over the top; let stand for 5 minutes to soften. Meanwhile, taste and season the ragù with salt and pepper, then remove and discard the bay. Stir in the softened gelatin until fully dissolved.

In a large pot, bring 3 quarts water to a boil. Add 2 teaspoons salt and the pasta, then cook, stirring occasionally, until just shy of al dente. Reserve ½ cup of the cooking water, then drain.

In the same pot over medium, bring 2 cups of the ragù to a simmer, stirring occasionally; reserve the remaining ragù for another use. Add the tagliatelle and cook, stirring occasionally, until the pasta is al dente, about 2 minutes; add cooking water as needed to thin. Off heat, taste and season with salt and pepper. Serve drizzled with oil (if using) and sprinkled with Parmesan.

Spaghetti with Lemon Pesto

Start to finish: 25 minutes
Servings: 4

This pasta dish is modeled on the spaghetti al pesto di limone that Giovanna Aceto made for us on her family's farm in Amalfi, Italy. The lemons commonly available in the U.S. are more acidic than Amalfi's lemons, so to make a lemon pesto that approximates the original, we use a little sugar to temper the flavor. For extra citrus complexity, we add lemon zest to the pasta cooking water; the oils from the zest lightly perfume the spaghetti, reinforcing the lemony notes of the pesto.

4 lemons

Kosher salt and ground black pepper

1½ teaspoons white sugar, divided

1 pound spaghetti

½ cup slivered almonds

1 ounce (without rind) Parmesan cheese, cut into rough 1-inch pieces, plus finely grated Parmesan to serve

⅓ cup extra-virgin olive oil, plus more to serve

2 tablespoons finely chopped fresh chives

Using a vegetable peeler (preferably a Y-style peeler), remove the zest from the lemons in long, wide strips; try to remove only the colored portion of the peel, not the bitter white pith just underneath. You should have about ⅔ cup zest strips.

In a large pot, combine 2 quarts water, 1½ teaspoons salt, 1 teaspoon of sugar and half of the zest strips. Bring to a boil and cook for 2 minutes, then remove and discard the zest. Add the spaghetti and cook until al dente. Reserve 1½ cups of the cooking water, then drain the pasta and return it to the pot.

Meanwhile, in a food processor, combine the remaining zest strips, the almonds, Parmesan, the remaining ½ teaspoon sugar and ¼ teaspoon each salt and pepper. Process until the mixture resembles coarse sand, 10 to 20 seconds. Add the oil and process just until the oil is incorporated (the mixture will not be smooth), about another 10 seconds; set aside until the pasta is ready.

To the spaghetti in the pot, add the pesto and ¾ cup of the reserved pasta water, then toss to combine; add more reserved pasta water as needed so the pesto coats the noodles. Toss in the chives. Taste and season with salt and pepper. Serve drizzled with additional oil and with additional grated Parmesan on the side.

Spaghetti with Shrimp, Tomatoes and White Wine

Start to finish: 45 minutes
Servings: 4 to 6

In Venice, Italy, cookbook author Marika Contaldo Seguso taught us to make a regional classic, scampi alla busara. Large, sweet, shell-on prawns are bathed in a sauce made with fresh tomatoes, a splash of white wine, smashed garlic cloves and a sprinkling of pepper flakes. She paired her scampi alla busara with al dente pasta, a terrifically delicious, though not strictly traditional, combination. We adapted Seguso's recipe using shelled shrimp in place of the prawns.

1 pound spaghetti

Kosher salt and ground black pepper

4 tablespoons extra-virgin olive oil, divided, plus more to serve

4 medium garlic cloves, smashed and peeled

1½ pounds extra-large shrimp (21/25 per pound), peeled (tails removed and reserved) and deveined

⅓ cup dry white wine

2 pounds ripe plum tomatoes, cored and chopped

1 cup lightly packed fresh basil, torn

2 teaspoons white sugar

½ teaspoon red pepper flakes

In a large pot, bring 3 quarts water to a boil. Add the spaghetti and 2 teaspoons salt; cook, stirring occasionally, until just shy of al dente. Reserve about 1 cup of the cooking water, then drain the pasta and return it to the pot; set aside.

In a 12-inch skillet over medium, heat 2 tablespoons of the oil until shimmering. Add the garlic and shrimp tails, then cook, stirring occasionally, until the garlic begins to brown, 3 to 4 minutes. Add the wine, bring to a simmer and cook, stirring, until it has reduced by about half, 2 to 3 minutes. Using tongs or a slotted spoon, remove and discard the garlic and shrimp tails.

Into the wine reduction, stir the tomatoes, half of the basil, the sugar, pepper flakes and ½ teaspoon each salt and black pepper. Bring to a simmer over medium-high, then reduce to medium and simmer, stirring occasionally, until the tomatoes are softened and jammy and the juices have fully evaporated, 12 to 15 minutes.

Add the shrimp and cook, stirring occasionally, until they begin to turn pink, about 2 minutes. Pour the mixture over the spaghetti in the pot, then add the remaining 2 tablespoons oil and ½ cup of the pasta water. Cook over medium, tossing with tongs, until the sauce clings to the spaghetti and the shrimp are cooked through, 3 to 4 minutes; add more cooking water 1 tablespoon at a time if the mixture looks dry.

Off heat, taste and season with salt and pepper, then stir in the remaining basil. Serve drizzled with additional oil.

Gnocchi with Pesto alla Genovese

Start to finish: 30 minutes
Servings: 4 to 6

We were taught to make pesto alla Genovese in its birthplace—Genoa, Italy, by chef Roberto Panizza. It traditionally is made in a mortar and pestle; we use a food processor for convenience but follow the tradition of processing ingredients separately to ensure we preserve the appropriate texture of each. Seek out true Italian Parmesan cheese, as well as pecorino Sardo, a sheep's milk cheese from Sardinia. If you can't find pecorino Sardo, the best substitute is manchego, a Spanish sheep's milk cheese. We've paired the pesto with gnocchi, a classic combination; either potato gnocchi (see recipe p. 22), "instant" gnocchi made with potato flakes (see recipe p. 29), gnocchi di farina (see recipe p. 26) or even store-bought gnocchi will do well, but the gnocchi must be just-cooked and warm because it will not be heated during the saucing process. If pasta is your preference, the recipe makes enough pesto to sauce 12 ounces of uncooked pasta.

1¾ ounces Parmesan cheese (without rind), chopped into rough 1-inch pieces

1 ounce pecorino Sardo cheese (without rind), chopped into rough 1-inch pieces (see headnote)

¼ cup pine nuts

2 medium garlic cloves, smashed and peeled

Kosher salt

⅓ cup extra-virgin olive oil

2½ ounces fresh basil (about 5 cups lightly packed)

2 pounds gnocchi, homemade or store-bought (see headnote)

In a food processor, process both cheeses until broken into rough marble-sized pieces, about 10 seconds, then pulse until they have the texture of coarse sand, 5 to 10 pulses, scraping the bowl as needed. Transfer to a small bowl.

In the food processor, combine the pine nuts, garlic and ¼ teaspoon salt. Process until a smooth, peanut butter–like paste forms, about 1 minute, scraping the bowl as needed. Add the cheeses and about ½ of the oil; process until mostly smooth, 10 to 20 seconds, scraping the bowl as needed; the mixture should hold together when pressed against the bowl with a silicone spatula.

Using a chef's knife, roughly chop the basil, then add to the processor. Pulse about 10 times, scraping the bowl several times, until the basil is finely chopped and well combined with the cheese mixture. Add the remaining oil and pulse just until incorporated, about 2 pulses. The pesto should be thick, creamy and spreadable.

Cook and drain the gnocchi according to your recipe or the package instructions, reserving about ¾ cup of the cooking water. (If using one of our recipes for homemade gnocchi, do not allow the drained gnocchi to fully cool before saucing, as they will not be reheated in the pesto.) Return the gnocchi to the pot. Add the pesto and ¼ cup of the reserved cooking water. Gently stir until the pesto coats the gnocchi, adding more reserved water if needed. Taste and season with salt and pepper.

Spaghetti Puttanesca

Start to finish: 25 minutes
Servings: 4

We think of puttanesca as a saucy dish built on anchovies. But in Naples, where it originates, two varieties of briny olives and pungent capers, not anchovies, give the dish bold savoriness that balances the sweetness of the tomatoes. We got a lesson in how to make it from Antonella Scala, who hosted pop-up dinners in her rooftop kitchen on the outskirts of modern Pompeii. We call for a generous amount of capers, which often are sold in small bottles or jars. When shopping, you will need to buy two 4-ounce bottles to get the ½ cup drained capers needed for this recipe.

Kosher salt and ground black pepper

12 ounces spaghetti

2 tablespoons extra-virgin olive oil, divided

3 medium garlic cloves, smashed and peeled

1 teaspoon red pepper flakes

½ cup pitted Kalamata olives, roughly chopped

½ cup pitted green olives, roughly chopped

½ cup (two 4-ounce bottles) drained capers, rinsed, patted dry and chopped

28-ounce can whole peeled tomatoes, drained, 1 cup juices reserved, tomatoes crushed by hand into small pieces

½ cup lightly packed fresh basil, chopped

1 ounce Parmesan or pecorino Romano cheese, grated (½ cup), plus more to serve

In a large pot, bring 2 quarts water to a boil. Add 1½ teaspoons salt and the spaghetti, then cook, stirring occasionally, for 5 minutes. Reserve 2 cups of cooking water, then drain and set aside.

In a 12-inch skillet over medium, heat 1 tablespoon of oil and the garlic cloves, then cook, stirring often, until the garlic is light golden brown, about 1 minute. Off heat, remove and discard the garlic. Add the pepper flakes, both types of olives and the capers, then cook over medium-high, stirring, until the capers begin to brown, about 1 minute. Add the tomatoes and cook, stirring occasionally, until most of the liquid has evaporated, 5 to 7 minutes.

Add the reserved tomato juice and 1 cup of the reserved cooking water; bring to a simmer. Add the pasta and toss to coat. Cover and cook, tossing occasionally, until the pasta is al dente and the sauce clings lightly to the noodles; add more cooking water if needed.

Remove from the heat, cover and let stand for 3 minutes. Stir in the basil, cheese and remaining 1 tablespoon olive oil. Taste and season with salt and black pepper. Serve topped with additional cheese.

Pasta all'Amatriciana

Start to finish: 30 minutes
Servings: 4

Amatriciana is a minimalist equation of pasta, tomatoes, guanciale and pecorino Romano cheese. In Rome, it's served with barely any sauce, as we learned from Mario Ive, retired artillery colonel in the Italian army and cookbook author. The cooking method—using as little liquid as possible when cooking the sauce—concentrates flavors, which coats the pasta nicely. We apply that principle for the pasta in this recipe, as well, cooking spaghetti in half the amount of water we usually use.

3 tablespoons extra-virgin olive oil, divided

3 ounces thinly sliced pancetta, finely chopped

10 medium garlic cloves, thinly sliced

½ teaspoon red pepper flakes

¾ cup dry white wine

14½-ounce can whole peeled tomatoes, drained, juices reserved, tomatoes crushed by hand into small pieces

1-ounce chunk pecorino Romano cheese, plus more finely grated, to serve

Kosher salt and ground black pepper

12 ounces spaghetti

In a 12-inch skillet over medium, heat 1 tablespoon of the oil until shimmering. Add the pancetta and cook, stirring, until well-browned and crisp, 5 to 7 minutes. Using a slotted spoon, transfer to a paper towel–lined plate and set aside.

Return the skillet to medium and add the garlic; cook, stirring, until light golden brown, about 2 minutes. Stir in the pepper flakes and cook until fragrant, about 30 seconds. Add the wine, increase to medium-high and cook, stirring, until most of the liquid has evaporated, 5 to 7 minutes. Add the drained tomatoes and cook, stirring, until heated, about 2 minutes. Stir in 3 tablespoons of the reserved tomato juice, then remove from the heat.

Meanwhile, in a large pot, bring 2 quarts of water and the pecorino chunk to a boil, stirring occasionally to prevent the cheese from sticking to the pot. Stir in the pasta and 1 teaspoon salt. Cook, stirring often, until the pasta is just shy of al dente. Remove and discard the pecorino, then drain the pasta in a colander set in a large heat-safe bowl; reserve the cooking water.

Set the skillet over medium-high, stir in 1½ cups of the reserved pasta water and bring to a simmer. Add the drained pasta, tossing with tongs. Cook, stirring occasionally, until most of the liquid has been absorbed, 3 to 6 minutes.

Off heat, stir in the remaining 2 tablespoons oil, the pancetta and 2 teaspoons black pepper. Transfer to a serving bowl and serve with grated pecorino on the side.

Spaghetti with Clams

Start to finish: 35 minutes
Servings: 4

At Perduto, a canal-side restaurant in Venice, Italy, chef Gianpiero Turdo taught us how to make a regional pasta classic: bigoli con vongole (bigoli with clams). The al dente pasta, garlic, wine, parsley and briny clams were a seamless blend of complementary flavors and the deliciousness of the dish belied the ease with which it came together. Bigoli is a long, thick, round extruded noodle, sometimes made with whole-wheat flour, sometimes with eggs. In the U.S., easier-to-find spaghetti or bucatini are good substitutes. We prefer littleneck clams for this recipe, but Manila clams also work. Whichever variety you use, scrub the clams well to remove as much grit as possible.

12 ounces spaghetti or bucatini

Kosher salt and ground black pepper

3 tablespoons extra-virgin olive oil, plus more to serve

4 medium garlic cloves, smashed and peeled

¼ teaspoon red pepper flakes

1 cup dry white wine

3 pounds littleneck or Manila clams, scrubbed

½ cup finely chopped fresh flat-leaf parsley

Lemon wedges, to serve

In a large pot, bring 2 quarts water to a boil. Stir in the pasta and 1½ teaspoons salt, then cook, stirring occasionally, until just shy of al dente. Reserve about 2 cups of the cooking water, then drain; set aside.

In a large Dutch oven over medium-high, combine the oil and garlic; cook, stirring until the garlic is lightly browned, about 2 minutes. Add the pepper flakes and cook, stirring, until fragrant, about 30 seconds. Remove and discard the garlic. Stir in the wine, bring to a simmer and cook until reduced to about ¼ cup, 6 to 8 minutes.

Stir in the clams, cover and cook, stirring occasionally; as the clams open, transfer them to a large bowl. When all clams have opened, simmer the juices in the pot until reduced by half.

Add the pasta and any accumulated clam juices (but not the clams themselves) in the bowl to the pot. Cook, constantly stirring and tossing, until the pasta is al dente, 2 to 3 minutes, adding reserved pasta water as needed so the noodles are lightly sauced.

Off heat, stir in the parsley, then taste and season with salt and pepper. Return the clams and any remaining juices to the pot; toss to combine. Serve drizzled with additional oil and with lemon wedges on the side.

Rigatoni with Roman Broccoli Sauce

Start to finish: 35 minutes
Servings: 4

This is an adaptation of a pasta we had in Rome. There, cooks use the leaves that grow around heads of broccoli to make a flavorful sauce for pasta. In the U.S., most of the leaves are stripped off before broccoli is sold. Our recipe instead uses the stems, which are equally flavorful and produce a silky sauce. Baby spinach retains the color of the original recipe.

1 pound broccoli, stems and florets separated

Kosher salt and ground black pepper

1½ cups packed baby spinach

2 medium garlic cloves, chopped

4 tablespoons (½ stick) salted butter, cut into 4 pieces

1 tablespoon drained capers

½ teaspoon red pepper flakes

2 tablespoons finely grated lemon zest, divided

12 ounces rigatoni pasta

1 ounce pecorino Romano or Parmesan cheese, finely grated (½ cup), plus more to serve

In a large pot, bring 4 quarts water and 1 tablespoon salt to a boil. Peel the broccoli stems, reserving any leaves, and cut crosswise into ½-inch rounds. Add the stems and leaves to the boiling water and cook until fully tender, about 10 minutes. Stir in the spinach and cook until wilted, about 20 seconds. Using a slotted spoon, transfer the vegetables to a blender; reserve ½ cup of the cooking water. Keep the water at a boil.

Cut the broccoli florets into 1- to 1½-inch pieces. Add the florets to the boiling water and cook until crisp-tender, about 3 minutes. Using the slotted spoon, transfer to a colander and rinse under cold water until cooled. Again, keep the water at a boil.

To the blender, add the garlic, butter, capers, pepper flakes, ¼ teaspoon salt, 1 tablespoon of the lemon zest and the reserved broccoli cooking water. Puree until smooth and bright green, about 30 seconds. Taste and season with salt and pepper.

Stir the rigatoni into the boiling water and cook until al dente. Reserve ½ cup of the cooking water, then drain. Return the pasta to the pot and add the broccoli florets, the broccoli puree, ¼ cup of the reserved cooking water, the remaining 1 tablespoon lemon zest and the cheese.

Cook over medium, stirring constantly, until the sauce thickens slightly and the pasta is well coated, 1 to 2 minutes. Remove from the heat. Taste and season with salt and pepper.

Penne with Eggplant, Tomatoes and Ricotta Salata

Start to finish: 50 minutes
Servings: 4

This classic Sicilian dish of eggplant and pasta in tomato sauce, known as pasta alla Norma, is said to take its name from a 19th-century Bellini opera. The eggplant usually is fried before being added to the sauce, but we roast it to concentrate its flavor and condense its porous texture. The eggplant is in the oven for about 30 minutes unattended; use that time to prep the other ingredients and simmer the tomatoes to make the sauce. Ricotta salata is a firm cheese with a milky, salty flavor. Do not substitute fresh ricotta; a mild feta is a more appropriate substitute.

1-pound eggplant, peeled and cut into ¾-inch cubes

6 tablespoons extra-virgin olive oil, divided

Kosher salt

8 medium garlic cloves, finely chopped

½ teaspoon red pepper flakes

2 pints cherry or grape tomatoes

2 tablespoons white balsamic vinegar

12 ounces penne or mezze rigatoni pasta

½ cup lightly packed fresh basil, roughly chopped

2 ounces ricotta salata cheese, shredded on the large holes of a box grater

Heat the oven to 475°F with a rack in the upper-middle position. Line a rimmed baking sheet with kitchen parchment. In a large bowl, toss the eggplant with 4 tablespoons oil and ¾ teaspoon salt. Distribute in an even layer on the prepared baking sheet and roast until browned and tender, 30 to 35 minutes, stirring once halfway through. Remove from the oven and set aside.

While the eggplant roasts, in a 12-inch skillet over medium-high, heat the remaining 2 tablespoons oil until shimmering. Add the garlic and pepper flakes and cook, stirring, until fragrant, about 30 seconds. Add the tomatoes and ¾ teaspoon salt, then cover and cook, occasionally shaking the pan, until the tomatoes begin to release their liquid, about 1 minute. Stir in the vinegar, then use the back of a large spoon to crush the tomatoes. Cover, reduce to medium and cook, stirring occasionally, until the mixture breaks down into a lightly thickened sauce, 8 to 9 minutes. Remove from the heat and cover to keep warm.

In a large pot, bring 4 quarts of water to a boil. Stir in the pasta and 1 tablespoon salt, then cook, stirring occasionally, until the pasta is just shy of al dente. Reserve about ½ cup of the cooking water, then drain and return the pasta to the pot.

Add the eggplant, tomato sauce and ¼ cup of the reserved pasta water to the pasta. Cook over medium, stirring, until the sauce begins to cling to the pasta, 2 to 3 minutes. Stir in half of the basil, then taste and season with salt and pepper. Serve sprinkled with the remaining basil and the ricotta salata.

Spaghetti with Tuna and Mushrooms

Start to finish: 40 minutes
Servings: 6

This is our take on the Italian dish known as spaghetti alla carrettiera ("in the style of cart drivers"). We were inspired by the Roman version, which uses tomatoes, tuna and dried porcini mushrooms, but we use cremini or white mushrooms. Olive oil-packed tuna is traditional; the oil often is added to the sauce, as we've done. Chopped fresh flat-leaf parsley is a nice garnish that adds grassy freshness.

1 pound spaghetti or linguine

Kosher salt and ground black pepper

3 tablespoons extra-virgin olive oil, plus more to serve

8 ounces cremini or white mushrooms, trimmed and sliced

1 small red onion, halved and thinly sliced

4 medium garlic cloves, minced

¼ to ½ teaspoon red pepper flakes

Two 5-ounce cans olive oil-packed tuna, drained, oil reserved

14½-ounce can diced tomatoes

In a large pot, bring 4 quarts water to a boil. Add the pasta and 1 tablespoon salt, then cook, stirring occasionally, until al dente. Reserve 1 cup of the cooking water, then drain; set aside.

In the same pot over medium-high, heat the oil until shimmering. Add the mushrooms, onion and ½ teaspoon salt. Cook, stirring occasionally, until the liquid released by the mushrooms has evaporated and the mushrooms are browned, 5 to 6 minutes. Add the garlic, pepper flakes, ½ teaspoon black pepper and the reserved oil from the tuna; cook, stirring, until fragrant, about 30 seconds. Stir in the tomatoes with juices and ½ cup of the reserved cooking water. Bring to a simmer and cook, stirring occasionally, until a spatula leaves a trail when drawn through the mixture, about 5 minutes.

Add the pasta and tuna. Using tongs, toss until the pasta is heated through and the sauce clings lightly, breaking up any large tuna chunks and adding more cooking water as needed if the mixture looks dry. Off heat, taste and season with salt and black pepper. Serve drizzled with additional oil.

Gnocchi alla Romana

Start to finish: 2¼ hours (30 minutes active)
Servings: 4 to 6

Despite sharing a name, these dumplings are quite different from the more widely known potato-based gnocchi. Instead, they're made from a stovetop semolina dough that's spread into a thinnish layer on a baking sheet and chilled until firm. The slab then is cut into rounds or squares, doused in butter and cheese and baked. The dumplings' cheesy, delicately crisp exteriors and pillowy-soft insides make them deeply satisfying. Be sure to thoroughly chill the dough before slicing and shingling the gnocchi in the baking dish—they're far easier to handle when cold.

6 tablespoons salted butter, cut into 1-tablespoon pieces, plus 2 tablespoons salted butter, melted

5 cups whole milk

1¾ cups semolina flour

3 ounces Parmesan cheese, finely grated (1½ cups)

¾ teaspoon grated nutmeg

Kosher salt and ground black pepper

2 large eggs, lightly beaten

Rub a 1-tablespoon piece of butter over a rimmed baking sheet (approximately 13-by-18 inches) and a 9-by-13 inch baking dish; set aside.

In a large saucepan over medium, heat the milk to just below a simmer. While whisking constantly, slowly stream in the semolina. Switch to a silicone spatula or wooden spoon and cook, stirring often, until the mixture is thick, slightly elastic and pulls away from the sides of the pan, 6 to 8 minutes.

Off heat, add the remaining 5 tablespoon-size pieces of butter, half of the Parmesan, the nutmeg and 1¼ teaspoons each salt and pepper; stir until the butter is melted and incorporated. Add the eggs, then stir vigorously until well combined.

Pour the mixture into the center of the prepared baking sheet and, using a spatula, spread into an even layer all the way to the edges. Refrigerate, uncovered, until fully chilled, about 1 hour; for longer storage, once chilled, cover with plastic wrap and refrigerate up to 24 hours.

About 20 minutes before you plan to bake, heat the oven to 425°F with a rack in the upper-middle position.

Remove the baking sheet from the refrigerator. Using a dinner knife, cut the semolina slab into quarters lengthwise and sixths crosswise to make 24 rough squares. Remove the pieces from the baking sheet (a thin metal spatula works well) and arrange them in the prepared baking dish, shingling them to fit. Brush the melted butter onto the gnocchi, then sprinkle with the remaining Parmesan.

Bake until the cheese is melted and the gnocchi are browned in spots, 30 to 35 minutes. Cool for about 10 minutes before serving.

Stir-Fries

Spicy Glass Noodles with Ground Pork

Start to finish: 30 minutes
Servings: 4

The unique name of this Sichuan classic—ants climbing a tree—is a direct translation from the Mandarin. The little bits of pork clinging to the noodles are said to resemble ants climbing a tree. Thin and wiry, glass noodles go by a few different names, including cellophane noodles, bean threads and sai fun. Chinese chili bean paste called toban djan (sometimes spelled doubanjiang) provides spicy heat as well as deep savoriness and umami. Look for it sold in jars in the international aisle of the supermarket or in an Asian grocery store. If you are unable to source toban djan, 2 teaspoons red miso plus 3 teaspoons chili-garlic sauce is a decent approximation. If you like, drizzle the noodles with sesame oil before serving and offer steamed greens alongside to complete the meal.

Place the noodles in a medium heatproof bowl and pour in boiling water to cover. Let stand until the noodles are pliable, about 15 minutes, then drain in a colander and rinse under running cold water. Using kitchen shears, snip the noodles in several places to cut them into shorter lengths. In a small bowl, stir together the pork, the 2 teaspoons soy sauce and ½ teaspoon pepper.

In a 12-inch skillet over medium-high, combine the pork mixture and the oil. Cook, breaking the meat into tiny bits, until it is no longer pink, 2 to 4 minutes. Add the scallion whites, ginger, garlic, chili(es) and chili bean paste; cook, stirring, until fragrant, about 1 minute. Stir in the remaining 1 tablespoon soy sauce and the sugar, then add the broth and bring to a boil. Add the noodles to the skillet and cook, stirring often, until the noodles have absorbed the liquid and the bits of pork cling to the strands, 3 to 5 minutes.

Off heat, stir in the scallion greens. Taste and season with salt and pepper.

---

4 ounces glass noodles (see headnote)

Boiling water, for soaking the noodles

8 ounces ground pork

2 teaspoons plus 1 tablespoon soy sauce, divided

Kosher salt and ground black pepper

2 teaspoons grapeseed or other neutral oil

2 scallions, thinly sliced, whites and greens reserved separately

1 tablespoon minced fresh ginger

2 medium garlic cloves, minced

1 or 2 Fresno or jalapeño chilies, stemmed, seeded and chopped

1 tablespoon chili bean paste (toban djan)

1 teaspoon white sugar

½ cup low-sodium chicken broth

Thai Stir-Fried Rice Noodles with Chicken and Basil

Start to finish: 35 minutes
Servings: 4 to 6

The Thai name for this dish, kway teow pad kee mao gai, translates roughly as "drunkard's stir-fried noodles with chicken." It supposedly started out as a spicy, noodle-less stir-fry created to satiate the appetites of drinkers. At some point, noodles were introduced to the mix and the dish is now a ubiquitous offering in many Thai restaurants. We've found that dried rice stick noodles about ¼ inch wide are available in most supermarkets and work well in the dish. If you can find holy basil, it's the best type to use here. But even if made with Mediterranean basil, this noodle stir-fry is delicious.

8 ounces dried rice stick noodles (see headnote)

Boiling water, to soak the noodles

3 tablespoons grapeseed or other neutral oil

12 ounces boneless, skinless chicken breasts, sliced crosswise about ¼ inch thick

2 teaspoons plus 1 tablespoon fish sauce, divided

1 teaspoon plus 1 tablespoon oyster sauce, divided

1 tablespoon soy sauce

1 tablespoon packed brown sugar

3 medium shallots, halved and thinly sliced lengthwise

2 Fresno or jalapeño chilies, stemmed, seeded and sliced into thin half rings

1 cup lightly packed fresh basil (see headnote), roughly torn

Place the noodles in a large heatproof bowl and add boiling water to cover. Let stand, stirring once or twice and separating any strands that are sticking together, until the noodles are pliable, about 15 minutes, then drain. If the noodles are in very long strands, snip them with kitchen shears in several places to cut them into shorter lengths.

In a medium bowl, toss the chicken with the 2 teaspoons fish sauce and the 1 teaspoon oyster sauce. In a small bowl, stir together the remaining 1 tablespoon fish sauce, remaining 1 tablespoon oyster sauce, the soy sauce, sugar and ¼ cup water.

In a 12-inch nonstick skillet over medium-high, heat the oil until shimmering. Add the chicken in a single layer and cook, stirring only once or twice, until lightly browned, 2 to 4 minutes.

Add the shallots and chilies; cook, stirring occasionally, until softened and beginning to brown, about 2 minutes. Add the noodles and sauce mixture; cook, stirring and tossing, until the noodles are tender, about 5 minutes. Off heat, toss in the basil.

Peruvian Stir-Fried Chicken and Noodles

Start to finish: 40 minutes
Servings: 4

This salty-sweet chicken and noodle stir-fry is our take on tallarin saltado, a chifa staple. Born of Chinese migration to Peru in the late 19th century, chifa cuisine combines South American and East Asian flavors and ingredients. In this recipe, garlicky chicken and peppers are coated in a soy- and oyster sauce-based glaze, then tossed with thin, chewy noodles. Though traditionally made with wine vinegar, we loved the fruity yet mellow acidity added by balsamic. An optional Fresno chili—our stand-in for Peru's floral-hot ají amarillos—provides a touch of bright heat.

8 ounces spaghetti

Kosher salt and ground black pepper

3 tablespoons oyster sauce

2 tablespoons soy sauce

2 tablespoons balsamic vinegar

3 tablespoons grapeseed oil or other neutral oil

1 pound boneless, skinless chicken thighs, trimmed and cut into ¾-inch strips

1 medium red onion, halved and sliced into ½-inch wedges

3 medium garlic cloves, thinly sliced

1 medium red, yellow or orange bell pepper, stemmed, seeded and thinly sliced

1 Fresno or jalapeño chili, stemmed, halved and thinly sliced

2 tablespoons lime juice, plus wedges to serve

¼ cup lightly packed fresh cilantro

In a large saucepan, bring 2 quarts water to a boil. Add the pasta and 1 tablespoon salt, then cook, stirring occasionally, until just shy of al dente. Reserve about ½ cup of the cooking water, then drain. In a small bowl, stir together the oyster sauce, soy sauce and vinegar; set aside.

In a 12-inch skillet over medium-high, heat the oil until barely smoking. Add the chicken, onion and garlic, distributing the ingredients evenly, then sprinkle with ¼ teaspoon each salt and pepper. Cook, without stirring, until the chicken is well browned on the bottom and releases easily from the pan, about 4 minutes. Add the oyster sauce mixture and cook, stirring and scraping up any browned bits, until the sauce is syrupy, 3 to 4 minutes. Add the bell pepper and chili; cook, stirring occasionally, until beginning to soften, about 2 minutes.

Add the pasta and stir to combine. Add the reserved pasta water and cook, tossing constantly, until the noodles are al dente, 2 to 3 minutes. Off heat, stir in the lime juice. Taste and season with salt and pepper. Serve sprinkled with cilantro and lime wedges on the side.

Korean Stir-Fried Noodles with Mushrooms and Spinach

Start to finish: 35 minutes
Servings: 4 to 6

Chap chae, also spelled japchae, is a much-loved Korean noodle dish with a savory-sweet and often sesame-centric flavor profile. The correct type of noodle to use is dang myun, or Korean sweet potato noodles (so called because they are made from sweet potato starch). The uncooked strands are tough, wiry and grayish, but with hydration and heat, they become translucent, take on a delightfully springy, bouncy texture and do an excellent job of absorbing seasonings. In all likelihood, dang myun will require a trip to the Asian market, but it's worth seeking out. Chap chae is best served hot, but it's delicious even at room temperature.

8 ounces sweet potato noodles (dang myun; see headnote)

Boiling water, for soaking noodles

⅓ cup soy sauce, plus more to taste

2½ tablespoons toasted sesame oil

2½ tablespoons packed light brown sugar

Kosher salt and ground black pepper

3 tablespoons grapeseed or other neutral oil, divided

1 medium yellow onion, halved and thinly sliced

8 ounces shiitake mushrooms, stemmed, thinly sliced

6 medium garlic cloves, minced

5-ounce container baby spinach

4 scallions, cut into 1-inch lengths

2 tablespoons sesame seeds, toasted

Place the noodles in a large heatproof bowl and add boiling water to cover. Let stand, stirring once or twice, until the noodles are pliable, 5 to 10 minutes, then drain. If the noodles are in very long strands, snip them with kitchen shears in several places to cut them into shorter lengths.

In a small bowl, combine the soy sauce, sesame oil, sugar and ¾ teaspoon pepper. Stir until the sugar dissolves; set aside.

In a 12-inch skillet over medium-high, heat 1 tablespoon neutral oil until barely smoking. Add the onion and cook, stirring often, until golden and charred along the edges, about 4 minutes. Transfer to a medium bowl.

Return the skillet to medium-high, and heat the remaining 2 tablespoons oil until shimmering. Add the mushrooms and ¼ teaspoon salt; cook, stirring often, until softened and browned, about 2 minutes. Add the garlic and cook, stirring, until fragrant, about 30 seconds. Transfer to the bowl with the onion.

To the skillet, add the soy mixture and 1½ cups water. Bring to a boil over medium-high, scraping up any browned bits. Add the noodles, then stir in the spinach a handful at a time, allowing the leaves to wilt slightly before adding more. Cook, stirring and tossing with tongs, until the noodles are tender and have absorbed the liquid, 5 to 8 minutes.

Add the scallions and the onion-mushroom mixture; cook, stirring and tossing, until heated through, about 2 minutes. Off heat, stir in the sesame seeds. Taste and season with additional soy sauce, if needed.

Japanese Fried Noodles with Bacon and Cabbage

Start to finish: 35 minutes
Servings: 4

Salty-sweet, umami-packed Japanese stir-fried noodles called yakisoba are a wildly popular type of casual comfort food. At home, yakisoba can be made "instantly," much like instant ramen, or it can be prepared using kits sold in the refrigerator section of the supermarket. We prefer to boil (non-instant) dried ramen, which is sometimes sold as bricks (similar to instant ramen) and sometimes as spaghetti-straight strands, then create our own seasoning mix. If you're able to purchase a yakisoba kit, discard the seasoning packet and use only the noodles, which are precooked (if using noodles from a kit, you'll need 10 to 12 ounces). If Italian pasta is the only type of noodle available, see _How to "Ramenize" Pasta_ below.

8 ounces non-instant dried ramen noodles or 10 to 12 ounces precooked ramen noodles (see headnote)

2 teaspoons grapeseed or other neutral oil

¼ cup soy sauce

3 tablespoons ketchup

2 tablespoons Worcestershire sauce

Ground black pepper

8 ounces bacon, chopped

2 medium shallots, halved and thinly sliced

1 medium red bell pepper, stemmed, seeded and thinly sliced

4 ounces green cabbage, cut into 1-inch pieces (about 2 cups)

Toasted nori snacks, crumbled or cut into thin strips, to serve

Pickled ginger, to serve

If using dried ramen, in a large pot, bring 4 quarts water to a boil. Add the ramen and cook, stirring occasionally, until tender, then drain in a colander. Rinse under running cool water until cool to the touch, then drain again. Drizzle with the oil and toss to coat; set aside. If using precooked ramen, rinse the noodles in a colander under warm running water, gently separating the strands with your fingers. Drizzle with the oil and toss to coat; set aside.

In a small bowl, stir together the soy sauce, ketchup, Worcestershire sauce, ¼ cup water and ½ teaspoon pepper; set aside.

In a 12-inch skillet over medium-high, cook the bacon, stirring occasionally, until beginning to crisp and brown, 4 to 6 minutes. Add the shallots, bell pepper and cabbage. Cook, stirring occasionally, until the shallots are lightly browned and the peppers and cabbage are just wilted, 5 to 8 minutes.

Add the noodles and soy sauce mixture. Cook over medium, continuously stirring and tossing, until the pan is dry, 3 to 5 minutes. Serve sprinkled with the nori and with pickled ginger on the side.

How to "Ramenize" Pasta

By boiling Italian pasta in water alkalized with baking soda, it's possible to mimic the firm, chewy texture of ramen noodles. In a large pot, bring 2 quarts water to a boil. Add 4 teaspoons baking soda and 10 ounces vermicelli. Cook, stirring occasionally, until tender. Drain the noodles in a colander. Rinse under cold running water, tossing well, until fully cooled, then drain again.

Pad Thai with Shrimp

Start to finish: 1 hour
Servings: 4

Across Bangkok, we tasted more than a dozen versions of pad Thai to understand the iconic noodle stir-fry and find a way to make the dish doable in American home kitchens, complete with its thrilling spicy-sour-salty-sweet profile. Based on lessons from numerous Thai cooks, we developed a recipe that delivers fantastic results—perfectly balanced flavors and the layers of contrasting textures that define great pad Thai. Suwan Pimtatong, cook at Hot Shoppe Restaurant, showed us how to build complexity and umami richness without the use of dried shrimp, a common pad Thai ingredient that isn't always easy to source in U.S. supermarkets. Additionally, we were able to achieve nuances of wok hei, or the hard-to-describe and even more difficult to attain (on a home cooktop) hints of smokiness that come from stir-frying in a wok over a raging-hot fire. The key is to add ingredients in batches to prevent the temperature of the wok from dropping precipitously. A few pointers for success: A 12- to 14-inch wok is essential, ideally one made of carbon steel that is well seasoned and conducts heat quickly. Use a neutral oil with a high smoke point; grapeseed or safflower is a good choice. Each time oil is heated in the empty wok, be sure it is smoking-hot before adding any ingredients. Use the cooking times as guidelines, don't take them as scripture, as burner output and heat-conduction properties of woks can differ greatly. Finally, be sure to have all ingredients and equipment, including a serving dish, ready before you head to the stovetop. Once cooking begins, it demands your full attention and is done in a matter of minutes.

10 ounces ¼-inch wide rice noodle sticks

2 tablespoons tamarind pulp

⅓ cup boiling water

2½ tablespoons packed light brown sugar or grated palm sugar

2 tablespoons oyster sauce

2 tablespoons soy sauce

1½ tablespoons fish sauce

1 cup bean sprouts

1 cup lightly packed fresh chives or slender scallions cut into 1-inch lengths

½ cup roasted peanuts, chopped

4 tablespoons grapeseed or safflower oil (see headnote), divided

12 ounces medium (41/50 per pound) shrimp, peeled (tails removed) and deveined

1 medium shallot, halved and thinly sliced

3 medium garlic cloves, minced

½ to ¾ teaspoon red pepper flakes

2 large eggs, beaten

Lime wedges, to serve

Fresh chilies in vinegar, to serve (optional, see recipe facing page)

Place the noodles in a large bowl and add hot water to cover (the water should feel hot to the touch, but should not be scalding). Let stand, stirring once or twice to separate any strands that are sticking together, for about 30 minutes; the noodles will become pliable but will not fully soften.

Meanwhile, in a small bowl, combine the tamarind pulp and boiling water; stir with a fork to break up the pulp. Cover and let stand for about 30 minutes. Strain the mixture through a fine-mesh sieve set over another small bowl; press on the solids and be sure to scrape the underside of the sieve to collect the pulp that clings; you should have about ¼ cup. Wipe out the small bowl used to hydrate the tamarind, then measure 3 tablespoons of the strained tamarind into it (reserve the remainder for another use). Add the sugar, oyster sauce, soy sauce and fish sauce. Stir until the sugar dissolves; place near the stove.

Drain the noodles in a colander. Shake the colander to remove excess water and set near the stove. In a medium bowl, toss together the bean sprouts, chives and peanuts; also set near the stove.

In a 12- to 14-inch wok over high, heat 1 tablespoon oil until smoking, swirling to coat. Add the shrimp and cook, stirring, until just beginning to curl and turn pink, 1 to 2 minutes; the shrimp will not be fully cooked. Transfer to a large plate; set aside. Wipe out the wok.

Return the wok to high and heat 2 tablespoons of the remaining oil until smoking, swirling to coat. Add the shallot, garlic and pepper flakes; cook, stirring, until fragrant and lightly browned, 20 to 30 seconds. Add the eggs (they will immediately puff) and cook, stirring from the edges inward, until the curds are barely set and shiny, 20 to 30 seconds.

Add half of the noodles. Cook, stirring, tossing and moving the noodles in a circular motion against the sides of the wok while also breaking up the eggs, until the noodles are dry, sizzling and are no longer stark white in color, 1 to 1½ minutes. Drizzle 1 tablespoon of the remaining oil down the sides of the wok and add the remaining noodles; cook in the same way until the mixture is once again dry and sizzling.

Pour half of the sauce mixture down the sides of the wok; it should bubble immediately and begin to thicken. Cook, tossing and moving the noodles in a circular motion against the sides of the wok, until the liquid is absorbed, about 30 seconds. Add the remaining sauce mixture and cook in the same way.

Add the shrimp (discard any accumulated juices) and half of the bean sprout mixture. Cook, stirring, until the shrimp are opaque throughout and the sprouts are just wilted, 1 to 2 minutes. Taste the noodles; if they are still too firm, drizzle in water 2 tablespoons at a time and cook, stirring, until the noodles are tender. Toss in the remaining sprout mixture. Transfer to a platter and serve with lime wedges and chilies in vinegar (if using).

Pad Thai with Tofu

Cut **8 ounces firm or extra-firm tofu** into ½- to ¾-inch cubes. Place in a single layer on a plate lined with a double thickness of paper towels. Cover with additional paper towels, place another plate on top, then set a few cans or jars on top as weights; let stand while you soak the noodles, prepare the tamarind and mix the sauce ingredients. Follow the recipe, substituting the tofu for the shrimp and stir-frying until the tofu is golden brown on all sides, about 3 minutes, setting it aside, then returning it to the wok as with the shrimp.

Pad Thai with Ground Pork

Follow the recipe, omitting the shrimp. When the shallot, garlic and pepper flakes are fragrant and lightly browned, add **8 ounces ground pork**; cook, stirring and breaking the pork into small bits, until the meat is lightly browned, 2 to 3 minutes. Make a clearing in the center of the mixture and add the eggs to the clearing, then continue with the recipe.

Fresh Chilies in Vinegar (Prik Nam Som)

Start to finish: 10 minutes
Makes about ¼ cup

In a small bowl or glass container, stir together **¼ cup unseasoned rice vinegar, 1 Fresno or serrano chili** (stemmed and sliced into thin rounds) and a **pinch kosher salt.** Cover and set aside until ready to use or refrigerate for up to 3 days.

Shanghai-Style Fried Noodles

Start to finish: 40 minutes
Servings: 4

The noodles in Shanghai fried noodles, or cu chao mian, are thick, chewy and wheaty, and they give the simply seasoned stir-fry much of its appeal. Japanese udon is similar in appearance and texture, and is easier to find in dried form in supermarkets. There is no sauce to speak of in this stir-fry—the noodles absorb the flavorings and in doing so take on a brownish hue. Oyster sauce is not a typical ingredient in Shanghai fried noodles, but it brings some sweetness along with loads of umami. The balsamic vinegar may also seem like an odd ingredient, but it's a great stand-in for malty, subtly sweet Chinese black vinegar that's made from rice.

2 teaspoons plus ¼ cup soy sauce, divided

2 teaspoons Shaoxing wine or dry sherry

2 teaspoons white sugar

1 teaspoon cornstarch

6- to 8-ounce boneless pork loin chop, sliced crosswise in ⅛-inch slices

2 tablespoons oyster sauce

1 tablespoon balsamic vinegar or Chinese black vinegar

Ground white pepper

10 ounces dried udon noodles

2 teaspoons toasted sesame oil

2 tablespoons grapeseed or other neutral oil

8 ounces baby bok choy, trimmed and quartered lengthwise

In a medium bowl, whisk together the 2 teaspoons soy sauce, the sherry, sugar and cornstarch. Add the pork and toss to coat; set aside. In a small bowl, combine the remaining ¼ cup soy sauce, oyster sauce, vinegar and ½ teaspoon white pepper; set aside.

In a large pot, bring 4 quarts water to a boil. Add the noodles and cook, stirring occasionally, until just shy of tender. Drain in a colander and rinse under cold water, tossing well, until cool to the touch. Drain again, shaking the colander to remove as much water as possible. Drizzle with the sesame oil and toss to coat; set aside.

In a 12-inch skillet over medium-high, heat the neutral oil until shimmering. Add the pork in an even layer and cook, stirring occasionally, until lightly browned, 1 to 2 minutes. Using a slotted spoon, transfer the pork to a plate.

To the now-empty skillet, add the bok choy; cook, stirring often, until the leaves are wilted and the stems are translucent, about 2 minutes.

Add the noodles and soy mixture. Cook, stirring often, until the noodles have absorbed most of the liquid, 3 to 4 minutes. Add the pork and any accumulated juices. Cook, tossing, until the noodles are dry, 1 to 2 minutes. Off heat, taste and season with white pepper.

Savory-Sweet Stir-Fried Noodles and Vegetables

Start to finish: 40 minutes
Servings: 4 to 6

These savory-sweet noodles are a riff on Indonesian mee goreng. Stir-fried red bell peppers and cabbage add texture and color to the tangle of chewy-tender noodles that get flavorful browning in a hot skillet. Look for fresh yellow Asian wheat noodles, often sold as lo mein or oil noodles, in the refrigerated section of the supermarket near the tofu. For spiciness and a little acidity, offer sambal oelek (or chili-garlic sauce) and lime wedges on the side.

1 pound fresh yellow Asian wheat noodles (see headnote)

Kosher salt and ground black pepper

1 teaspoon plus 3 tablespoons grapeseed or other neutral oil, divided

½ medium head (6 ounces) napa cabbage, thinly sliced (about 5 cups)

2 medium bell peppers, stemmed, seeded and thinly sliced

2 large shallots, halved and thinly sliced lengthwise

4 medium garlic cloves, minced

¼ cup low-sodium soy sauce

2 tablespoons oyster sauce

1 tablespoon packed brown sugar

Thinly sliced scallions, to serve

In a large pot, bring 2 quarts water to a boil. Add the noodles and cook until just shy of al dente, 2 to 3 minutes. Drain, rinse under running cold water until fully cooled, then drain again. Toss with 1 teaspoon of oil; set aside.

In a 12-inch nonstick skillet over medium-high, heat 1 tablespoon of the remaining oil until shimmering. Add the cabbage, peppers, shallots and ¼ teaspoon each salt and pepper; cook, stirring occasionally, until well browned, 6 to 7 minutes. Add the garlic and cook, stirring, until fragrant, about 30 seconds. Transfer to a medium bowl.

In the same skillet over medium-high, heat the remaining 2 tablespoons oil until barely smoking. Distribute the noodles in an even layer and cook without stirring until spotty brown, 2 to 3 minutes. Toss, redistribute in an even layer and cook without stirring for another 2 minutes.

Add the soy sauce, oyster sauce and sugar; cook, stirring, until only a small amount of glaze-like liquid remains, 1 to 2 minutes. Add the vegetables and cook, tossing to combine, until the pan is dry, about 2 minutes. Taste and season with salt and pepper. Serve sprinkled with scallions.

Filipino Stir-Fried Rice Vermicelli with Shrimp and Snow Peas

Start to finish: 35 minutes
Servings: 4 to 6

This is our version of Filipino pancit bihon, a stir-fry made with rice vermicelli (bihon). Though some versions are quite sparing in ingredients, the shrimp and vegetables make it hearty enough to serve as a main. A combination of fish sauce and soy sauce gives the noodles an umami-rich savoriness that's brightened at the end with lime juice. Be sure to use rice vermicelli that is thin and slightly squiggly; wide, flat rice noodles won't work here. The vermicelli needs only to be soaked and drained, making this an easy single-skillet dish.

8 ounces rice vermicelli (see headnote)

3 tablespoons grapeseed or other neutral oil, divided

1 pound medium shrimp (41/50 per pound), peeled and deveined, tails removed, patted dry

1 medium red onion, halved and thinly sliced

8 medium garlic cloves, minced

Kosher salt and ground black pepper

3 tablespoons fish sauce

2 tablespoons soy sauce

1 medium carrot, peeled, halved lengthwise, thinly sliced on the diagonal

4 ounces snow peas, trimmed and halved on the diagonal

4 teaspoons lime juice, plus lime wedges to serve

2 scallions, thinly sliced on the diagonal

1 serrano chili, stemmed, seeded and thinly sliced

Place the noodles in a large bowl and add water to cover. Let stand until the noodles are pliable, 10 to 15 minutes, then drain. If desired, use kitchen shears to snip the noodles in several places to cut them into shorter lengths.

In a 12-inch nonstick skillet over medium-high, heat 1 tablespoon oil until barely smoking. Add the shrimp in an even layer and cook without stirring until golden brown on the bottoms, 2 to 3 minutes. Transfer to a large plate and set aside.

In the same skillet over medium-high, heat the remaining 2 tablespoons oil until shimmering. Add the onion, garlic and ½ teaspoon pepper; cook, stirring, until fragrant, about 1 minute. Add 1½ cups water, the fish sauce and soy sauce, then bring to a boil. Add the noodles and carrot; cook, stirring and tossing often, until only a little liquid remains, 2 to 3 minutes.

Add the snow peas and shrimp with any accumulated juices. Cook, stirring and tossing, until the noodles are tender and dry, about 2 minutes.

Off heat, toss in the lime juice, half of the scallions and the chili. Taste and season with salt and pepper. Transfer to a serving dish and sprinkle with the remaining scallions. Serve with lime wedges.

Stir-Fried Rice Noodles with Beef and Broccolini

Start to finish: 30 minutes, plus marinating
Servings: 4

Beef chow fun is a Cantonese stir-fry of slippery wide-cut fresh rice noodles tangled with slices of tender-chewy beef, the whole thing tasting of wok hei, or the smoky-toasty flavor that comes from high-heat wok cooking. Since fresh rice noodles aren't easy to source and not every kitchen is equipped with a wide, flat-bottomed wok, we developed this recipe using widely available dried rice stick noodles (ones that measure about ½ inch wide are preferable) and do the stir-frying in a 12-inch skillet. The flavors and textures are different from the classic dish, but we think this rendition is delicious.

2 teaspoons plus ¼ cup soy sauce, divided, plus more to serve

2 teaspoons plus 2 tablespoons dry sherry or Shaoxing wine, divided

4 teaspoons toasted sesame oil, divided

3 teaspoons oyster sauce, divided

1 teaspoon cornstarch

Ground white pepper

12 ounces flank steak, cut with the grain into 2- to 3-inch pieces, then thinly sliced against the grain

8 ounces dried rice stick noodles (see headnote)

Boiling water, to soak the noodles

3 tablespoons grapeseed or other neutral oil

8 ounces Broccolini, halved lengthwise if thick

1 small yellow onion, halved and sliced about ¼ inch thick

4 medium garlic cloves, minced

4 scallions, cut into 2-inch lengths

In a medium bowl, whisk together 2 teaspoons soy sauce, 2 teaspoons sherry, 2 teaspoons sesame oil, 1 teaspoon oyster sauce, the cornstarch and ¼ teaspoon white pepper. Add the beef and toss to coat. Cover and refrigerate for at least 1 hour or for up to 4 hours.

Place the noodles in a large heatproof bowl and add boiling water to cover. Let stand, stirring once or twice and separating any strands that are sticking together, until the noodles are pliable, about 15 minutes, then drain. Toss with the remaining 2 teaspoons sesame oil and set aside.

In a small bowl, stir together the remaining ¼ cup soy sauce, the remaining 2 tablespoons sherry, the remaining 2 teaspoons oyster sauce, 3 tablespoons water and ½ teaspoon white pepper; set aside.

In a 12-inch skillet over medium-high, heat the grapeseed oil until barely smoking. Add the beef in an even layer and cook without stirring until well browned on the bottom and the pieces release easily from the skillet, about 3 minutes. Add the Broccolini, onion and garlic; cook, stirring and scraping up any browned bits, until the onion is lightly browned and the Broccolini is bright green, about 3 minutes.

Add the noodles, reduce to medium and cook, tossing to combine, for about 1 minute. Add the soy mixture and scallions; cook, tossing and scraping up any browned bits, until the noodles are tender and have absorbed the sauce and the Broccolini is tender-crisp, 3 to 5 minutes. Off heat, taste and season with additional soy sauce and white pepper.

Vietnamese Pan-Fried Noodles with Shrimp and Bok Choy

Start to finish: 40 minutes
Servings: 4

This is our version of mì xào giòn, or Vietnamese pan-fried noodles. The noodles are first boiled and drained, then pan-fried in a skillet into a crisp-crusted cake. A semi-saucy stir-fry of shrimp and mixed vegetables, seasoned with aromatics and fish sauce, goes on top, softening the noodles to crunchy-chewy deliciousness. Fresh Asian egg noodles that are similar in shape and size to spaghetti are the best type to use here. Look for them in the refrigerator case of the supermarket, usually sold alongside dumpling wrappers. If fresh egg noodles are not available, an equal amount of dried lo mein or non-instant ramen is a good substitute.

8 ounces fresh Asian egg noodles (see headnote)

6 tablespoons grapeseed or other neutral oil, divided

1 tablespoon cornstarch

1 pound large (26/30 per pound) shrimp, peeled (tails removed) and deveined

Kosher salt and ground black pepper

2-inch piece fresh ginger, peeled and cut into matchsticks (about 2 tablespoons)

6 medium garlic cloves, thinly sliced

4 scallions, whites thinly sliced, greens thinly sliced on the diagonal, reserved separately

4 ounces cremini mushrooms, trimmed and thinly sliced

1 medium carrot, peeled, halved and thinly sliced on the diagonal

1 cup low-sodium chicken broth

1½ tablespoons fish sauce

8 ounces baby bok choy, trimmed and cut crosswise into 1-inch pieces

In a large pot, bring 2 quarts water to a boil. Add the noodles and cook, stirring, until just shy of tender. Drain and rinse under cold water until cool. Drain again, removing as much water as possible; set aside.

In a 12-inch nonstick skillet over medium-high, heat 3 tablespoons oil until barely smoking. Add the noodles in an even layer and cook, undisturbed, until they release from the pan and are crisped and browned, about 5 minutes (check browning after about 3 minutes). Slide the noodles out of the pan onto a platter. Add 1 tablespoon of the remaining oil to the pan, then carefully flip the noodles back into the pan to cook the second side. Cook over medium until browned, about 6 minutes. Return the noodles to the platter and reserve the skillet.

In a small bowl, stir together the cornstarch and 2 tablespoons water; set aside. In a medium bowl, toss the shrimp with ¼ teaspoon each salt and pepper. In the same skillet over medium-high, heat 1 tablespoon of the remaining oil until shimmering. Add the shrimp and cook, stirring occasionally, until just pink on the exteriors but still translucent in the centers. Return the shrimp to the bowl in which they were seasoned.

To the same skillet over medium, add the remaining 1 tablespoon oil, the ginger, garlic, scallion whites, mushrooms and carrot. Cook, stirring, until fragrant, about 1 minute. Add the broth and fish sauce; bring to a simmer. Stir the cornstarch mixture to recombine, then stir it into the vegetable-broth mixture. Return to a simmer and cook, stirring, until the sauce is lightly thickened, about 1 minute.

Add the bok choy and shrimp along with any juices; cook, stirring, until the bok choy is tender-crisp and the shrimp are opaque throughout, about 2 minutes. Taste and season with salt and pepper. Scrape the mixture onto the noodles and sprinkle with scallion greens.

Lao Fried Noodles with Pork and Scallions

Start to finish: 35 minutes
Servings: 4

According to James Syhabout, Thai-Lao award-winning chef and author of "Hawker Fare," the rice noodle dish called khua mee is to Laos what pad Thai is to Thailand. Khua mee gets a distinctive flavor and aroma from sugar that is cooked until it caramelizes and takes on smoky, bittersweet notes. We use a trio of umami-rich sauces—fish, soy and oyster—to bring intensity and complexity to mild-tasting rice noodles. Look for flat rice sticks that are about ¼ inch wide, the same type used for pad Thai or Vietnamese pho. Crisp, savory-sweet fried shallots are a fantastic garnish for khua mee. Our recipe also yields shallot-infused oil for use in place of the neutral oil when making the stir-fry. If you're not up for frying shallots, not to worry—the noodles are delicious even without.

8 to 10 ounces dried rice stick noodles (see headnote)

Boiling water, to soak the noodles

2 large eggs

½ teaspoon plus 2 tablespoons fish sauce

3 tablespoons grapeseed or other neutral oil, divided

¼ cup white sugar

4 medium garlic cloves, minced

2 medium shallots, halved and thinly sliced

8 ounces ground pork

1 tablespoon oyster sauce

1 tablespoon soy sauce

1 bunch scallions, cut into 1-inch sections

1 cup bean sprouts

1 cup lightly packed fresh cilantro

Kosher salt

Lime wedges, to serve

Red pepper flakes, to serve

Fried shallots, to serve

Place the noodles in a large, heatproof bowl and add boiling water to cover. Let stand, stirring once or twice and separating any strands, until the noodles are pliable, about 15 minutes, then drain. If the noodles are long, snip them with kitchen shears into shorter lengths. Meanwhile, in a small bowl, beat the eggs with the ½ teaspoon fish sauce.

In a 12-inch nonstick skillet over medium, heat 2 tablespoons oil until barely smoking. Add the eggs and swirl to distribute in a thin layer. Cook until the surface is almost dry and the bottom is lightly browned, 30 to 60 seconds. Slide the omelet onto a cutting board; reserve the skillet. Let the omelet cool, then slice into thin ribbons.

In the same skillet over medium, combine the sugar with the remaining 1 tablespoon oil. Cook, stirring occasionally to dissolve, until the sugar begins to turn golden; cook, swirling the pan instead of stirring, until the caramel is amber, 2 to 4 minutes. Remove from the heat and add the garlic and shallots. Return to medium and cook, stirring, until fragrant, 45 to 60 seconds. Add the pork, oyster sauce, soy sauce and the remaining 2 tablespoons fish sauce. Cook, stirring and breaking the pork into small bits, until the meat is no longer pink, 2 to 3 minutes.

Add the noodles, scallions and 2 tablespoons water. Cook, tossing often, until the noodles are tender and have absorbed the liquid, about 3 minutes. If the pan is dry but the noodles are not yet tender, add more water, about 2 tablespoons at a time, and continue to cook.

Off heat, toss in the bean sprouts, half of the cilantro and half of the sliced omelet. Taste and season with salt. Transfer to a serving dish and garnish with the remaining cilantro and omelet. Serve with lime wedges, red pepper flakes and fried shallots (if using).

Fried Shallots and Shallot Oil

Start to finish: 15 minutes
**Makes about ⅔ cup fried shallots
and about 3 tablespoons infused oil**

In a nonstick 12-inch skillet over medium, combine
2 medium shallots (sliced into thin rings) and
¼ cup grapeseed or other neutral oil. Cook, stirring
occasionally, until the shallots are golden brown,
4 to 6 minutes. Drain in a fine-mesh sieve set over a
small heatproof bowl. Transfer the shallots to a
paper towel-lined plate; they will crisp as they cool.
The shallot-infused oil can be reserved for cooking
or for use in sauces or as a garnish.

Stir-Fried Noodles with Kimchi and Pork

Start to finish: 30 minutes
Servings: 4 to 6

This is an umami-packed, noodle-based version of another weeknight favorite, kimchi fried rice. Butter may seem out of place, but its richness smooths the edges and adds a velvety touch. If you like, sprinkle some furikake or crumble some crisp toasted nori onto the noodles just before serving.

10 ounces dried
udon noodles

2 teaspoons plus
2 tablespoons grapeseed
or other neutral oil

2 to 3 tablespoons
gochujang

2 tablespoons soy sauce

4 teaspoons white sugar

1 tablespoon kimchi juice,
plus 1½ cups drained
kimchi, roughly chopped

2 teaspoons toasted
sesame oil

8 ounces ground pork

1 bunch scallions, sliced
on the diagonal, whites and
greens reserved separately

2 tablespoons salted butter,
cut into 4 pieces

Kosher salt and ground
black pepper

3 tablespoons sesame
seeds, toasted

In a large pot, bring 4 quarts water to a boil. Add the noodles and cook, stirring occasionally, until tender. Drain in a colander and rinse under cold water until cool to the touch. Drain again and toss with the 2 teaspoons neutral oil, then set aside.

In a small bowl, whisk together the gochujang, soy sauce, sugar, kimchi juice, sesame oil and ¼ cup water; set aside.

In a 12-inch nonstick skillet over medium-high, heat the remaining 2 tablespoons neutral oil until shimmering. Add the pork and scallion whites; cook, breaking the meat into small bits, just until no longer pink, about 3 minutes. Increase to high and add the butter, kimchi and ½ teaspoon pepper. Cook, stirring often, until browned, about 2 minutes.

Add the noodles and toss, then add the gochujang mixture. Cook, stirring and tossing, until the noodles are heated through and the sauce clings, 2 to 3 minutes. Off heat, toss in the scallion greens and sesame seeds. Taste and season with salt and pepper.

One-Pan Pastas

Indian Vermicelli with Peas and Cilantro

Start to finish: 30 minutes
Servings: 4 to 6

Semiya upma, which inspired this recipe, is an Indian noodle dish commonly eaten for breakfast or as a snack. With bold flavors from spices, chili and herbs, we find it also makes a satisfying vegetarian dinner. This is a one-pot dish that doesn't require boiling then draining the noodles, so it can be on the table in well under an hour.

3 tablespoons grapeseed or other neutral oil

2 medium shallots, halved and thinly sliced

2-inch piece fresh ginger, peeled and minced (¼ cup)

1 tablespoon cumin seeds

1 teaspoon ground turmeric

1 Fresno or jalapeño chili, stemmed, seeded and minced

1 bunch cilantro, chopped, stems and leaves reserved separately

12 ounces vermicelli pasta, broken into 1-inch pieces

Kosher salt and ground back pepper

1 cup frozen peas, thawed

1 tablespoon grated lemon zest, plus 3 tablespoons lemon juice

1 cup roasted peanuts, chopped

In a large pot over medium, heat the oil until shimmering. Add the shallots and ginger, then cook, stirring occasionally, until the shallots are translucent, 2 to 3 minutes. Add the cumin and turmeric, then cook, stirring, until fragrant, about 30 seconds. Stir in the chili, cilantro stems and pasta. Add 3 cups water and ½ teaspoon each salt and pepper, then bring to a simmer over medium-high. Cover, reduce to medium-low and cook, stirring occasionally, until the pasta is al dente.

Off heat, add the cilantro leaves, peas, lemon zest and juice, and half the peanuts, then toss to combine. Taste and season with salt and pepper. Transfer to a serving dish and sprinkle with the remaining peanuts.

Pasta and Lentils
with Pomegranate Molasses

Start to finish: 1¼ hours (40 minutes active)
Servings: 4 to 6

This is our take on a classic Syrian dish called harak osbao. Brown lentils simmered with caramelized onions and a few spices make an earthy base in which fresh pasta is cooked, adding a silkiness to the dish. Sweet, sour and fruity pomegranate molasses (and pomegranate seeds, if using) and chopped fresh cilantro lift and brighten what might otherwise be a dish heavy with starchiness. Some versions of harak osbao are garnished with pieces of crisp fried flatbread that add a satisfying contrast in texture. We borrowed an idea from cookbook author and Middle Eastern food authority Anissa Helou, who suggests frying fresh pasta until crisp, then scattering the pieces on top just before serving.

¼ cup extra-virgin olive oil, plus more to serve

9-ounce container fresh fettuccine, noodles cut in half crosswise

1 medium red onion, halved and thinly sliced

Kosher salt and ground black pepper

¾ cup brown lentils, rinsed and drained

2 teaspoons ground cumin

1½ teaspoons ground coriander

2 tablespoons pomegranate molasses, plus more to serve

¾ cup lightly packed fresh cilantro, chopped

½ cup pomegranate seeds (optional)

In a 12-inch skillet, combine the oil and about a quarter of the pasta. Cook over medium-high, stirring often, until the pasta is crisp and golden brown, 3 to 5 minutes. Using a slotted spoon or tongs, transfer to a medium bowl, breaking any pieces that are very long; set aside.

To the oil remaining in the skillet, add the onion and ½ teaspoon salt. Cook over medium-high, stirring occasionally, until browned, 4 to 6 minutes. Transfer to a small bowl; set aside.

Add 4 cups water to the skillet and bring to a boil over medium-high, scraping up any browned bits. Stir in the lentils, cumin, coriander and ½ teaspoon each salt and pepper. Cover, reduce to medium and simmer, stirring occasionally, until the lentils are tender but still hold their shape, 32 to 36 minutes.

Uncover, add 2 cups water and bring to a boil over medium-high. Stir in the untoasted pasta and half of the cooked onions. Cook, uncovered and stirring occasionally, until the pasta is tender and the lentil mixture is creamy, 5 to 8 minutes.

Off heat, stir in the pomegranate molasses. Taste and season with salt and pepper. Transfer to a serving bowl and top with the remaining onion, the fried pasta, the cilantro and pomegranate seeds (if using).

Orecchiette with Coriander and Cherry Tomatoes

Start to finish: 25 minutes
Servings: 4 to 6

This recipe, inspired by an unusual pasta dish we tasted in Puglia, Italy, uses few ingredients but is packed with flavor. We layer in the warm, slightly citrusy flavor of coriander by blooming the spice in oil; most of it is simmered into the sauce and a couple teaspoons of the infused oil are drizzled on the finished dish. The cherry tomatoes, gently mashed after a few minutes of cooking, break down into a silky sauce that pairs perfectly with coin-sized, cup-shaped orecchiette pasta. Ricotta salata cheese is a milky, salty, crumbly cheese; grate it on the large holes of a box grater. If you can't find it, use an equal amount of queso fresco.

1 pound orecchiette pasta

Kosher salt and ground black pepper

2 tablespoons ground coriander

¼ cup extra-virgin olive oil

2 pints cherry or grape tomatoes

6 medium garlic cloves, thinly sliced

1 teaspoon grated lemon zest

1 ounce ricotta salata cheese, grated (¼ cup)

¼ cup lightly packed fresh basil, torn

In a large pot, bring 4 quarts water to a boil. Add the pasta and 1 tablespoon salt, then cook, stirring occasionally, until just shy of al dente. Reserve 1 cup of the cooking water, then drain the pasta; set aside.

Wipe dry the same pot, then set over medium, add the coriander and toast until fragrant, about 1 minute. Add the oil and cook until infused, about 2 minutes. Measure 2 teaspoons of the oil into a small bowl and set aside. Add the tomatoes and garlic to the pot, cover and cook, stirring once or twice, until softened and the oil has taken on a reddish hue, 4 to 6 minutes. Add ½ teaspoon salt and gently crush the tomatoes with a potato masher to release some of their liquid. Continue to cook, stirring to combine with the oil, for about 1 minute. Add the reserved cooking water, bring to a simmer over medium-high and cook, stirring occasionally, until the liquid is slightly reduced and the tomatoes are completely softened, about 3 minutes.

Add the pasta and cook, stirring often, until the pasta is al dente and has absorbed some of the liquid, 2 to 4 minutes. Stir in the lemon zest, then taste and season with salt and pepper. Transfer to a serving bowl, drizzle with the reserved oil and top with the cheese and basil.

Rigatoni with Tomato, Kale and Fontina

Start to finish: 35 minutes
Servings: 4 to 6

This one-pot pasta dish lets pantry ingredients do the heavy lifting. Fennel seeds, red pepper flakes and rosemary are bloomed in olive oil to release their essential oils before a full can of tomato paste—the bulk of the flavor backbone—goes into the mix. Cooking the paste until browned produces a vegetarian dish that is rich and savory. Diced fontina melts into the pasta, creating a creamy, unctuous texture; Taleggio also is a delicious option. We prefer lacinato kale, which sometimes is sold as Tuscan or dinosaur kale. Bunches vary in size; you'll need about 1 pound—one large bunch or two small ones—so if in doubt, toss the kale onto the produce scale at the supermarket.

1 pound rigatoni or ziti

Kosher salt and ground black pepper

1 large or 2 small bunches (1 pound) lacinato kale, stemmed and cut crosswise into 1-inch ribbons

3 tablespoons extra-virgin olive oil, plus more to serve

2 teaspoons fennel seeds

1 teaspoon red pepper flakes, plus more to serve

2 teaspoons chopped fresh rosemary

6-ounce can tomato paste (⅔ cup)

4 ounces fontina or Taleggio cheese (without rind), cut into ¼- to ½-inch cubes (about 1 cup)

In a large Dutch oven, bring 4 quarts water to a boil. Stir in the pasta and 1 tablespoon salt, then cook, stirring occasionally, until just shy of al dente. Working quickly, remove about 2 cups of the cooking water, then stir the kale into the pot and cook for another 1 minute. Drain and set the pasta-kale mixture aside.

In the same pot over medium, combine the oil, fennel seeds, pepper flakes and rosemary. Cook, stirring constantly, until fragrant and sizzling, 1 to 2 minutes. Add the tomato paste and ½ teaspoon each salt and black pepper, then cook, stirring often, until the paste browns and slightly sticks to the pot, 2 to 3 minutes.

Add 1½ cups of the reserved pasta water and bring to a simmer, scraping up any browned bits and stirring to dissolve the tomato paste. Add the pasta-kale mixture and cook, stirring, until the pasta is al dente and has absorbed the excess liquid, about 2 minutes; add more reserved water as needed so the pasta is silky and lightly sauced.

Off heat, stir in the cheese, then let stand for 1 to 2 minutes to allow the cheese to melt. Taste and season with salt and black pepper. Serve drizzled with additional oil and sprinkled with additional pepper flakes.

Farfalle with Creamy Carrots and Pancetta

Start to finish: 40 minutes
Servings: 4 to 6

This one-pot pasta dish is a riff on a unique recipe from "Thirty Minute Pasta" by Giuliano Hazan. A full pound of carrots plus a knob of butter, a shot of cream and a good dose of Parmesan combine to make a sauce that's flavorful and rich without being heavy. Salty pancetta and briny capers balance the natural sweetness of the carrots. To make quick work of carrot prep, you can use a food processor fitted with the shredding disk instead of a box grater.

4 ounces pancetta, finely chopped

1 pound carrots, peeled and shredded on the large holes of a box grater

2 tablespoons salted butter, cut into 2 pieces, divided

Kosher salt and ground black pepper

1 pound farfalle

1 cup lightly packed fresh flat-leaf parsley, finely chopped

1 ounce Parmesan cheese, finely grated (½ cup), plus more to serve

¼ cup heavy cream

2 tablespoons drained capers, minced

¼ teaspoon freshly grated nutmeg

In a large Dutch oven over medium, cook the pancetta, stirring occasionally, until lightly browned, about 5 minutes. Using a slotted spoon, transfer to a paper towel-lined plate; set aside. Add the carrots to the pot along with 1 tablespoon butter, 1 teaspoon salt and ½ teaspoon pepper. Cook, uncovered and stirring often, until the carrots begin to soften, 3 to 5 minutes.

Stir in 5 cups water and 1 teaspoon salt; bring to a simmer over medium-high. Add the pasta, submerging it in the water as much as possible. Cover and cook, stirring occasionally, until the pasta is al dente and almost dry; if the mixture is dry before the pasta is done, add about ½ cup water as needed.

Off heat, add the remaining 1 tablespoon butter, the parsley, Parmesan, cream, capers and nutmeg. Toss, adding additional water as needed so the pasta is lightly sauced. Taste and season with salt and pepper. Serve sprinkled with the pancetta and additional cheese.

Ziti with Tomatoes, Olives and Fried Capers

Start to finish: 45 minutes
Servings: 4 to 6

This pantry-centric pasta dish, full of high-impact southern Italian flavors, is made by simmering ziti directly in a briny, garlicky sauce. In addition to streamlining cooking and cleanup, the technique ensures the pasta is seasoned perfectly throughout. For added pops of flavor and crunchy texture, we fry capers until browned and crisp, then sprinkle them on just before serving. A finishing drizzle of olive oil and dusting of cheese bring a bit of body that ties everything together.

3 tablespoons extra-virgin olive oil, plus more to serve

¼ cup drained capers, patted dry

3 medium garlic cloves, thinly sliced

¼ to ½ teaspoon red pepper flakes

28-ounce can whole peeled tomatoes, crushed by hand

Kosher salt and ground black pepper

1 pound ziti

½ cup pitted black olives, roughly chopped

1 ounce Parmesan or pecorino Romano cheese, finely grated (½ cup), plus more to serve

½ cup lightly packed fresh basil, chopped

In a large pot over medium, heat the oil until shimmering. Add the capers and cook, stirring often, until crisp, 4 to 5 minutes. Remove the pot from the heat and, using a slotted spoon, transfer the capers to a paper towel-lined plate, leaving the oil in the pot.

Return the pot to medium and add the garlic. Cook, stirring occasionally, until golden brown, 1 to 2 minutes. Stir in the pepper flakes, tomatoes with juices and ½ teaspoon each salt and black pepper. Add 3 cups water and the pasta; stir to combine. Bring to a boil over medium-high, then reduce to medium, cover and cook, stirring occasionally, until the pasta is al dente.

Off heat, stir in the olives and Parmesan. Cover and let stand for 5 minutes. Add the basil and stir vigorously, then taste and season with salt and black pepper. Serve sprinkled with the fried capers and additional cheese, as well as drizzled with additional oil.

Pasta with Cauliflower, Garlic and Toasted Breadcrumbs

Start to finish: 25 minutes
Servings: 4

This pasta dish is a true one-pot dinner. We don't boil the noodles separately—rather, we add them to the pot along with the cauliflower and just enough water to cook both through. Toasted breadcrumbs sprinkled on just before serving offer a welcome textural contrast. We prefer Japanese-style panko over standard dry breadcrumbs for their light, airy texture that, when toasted, takes on a remarkable crispness.

4 tablespoons extra-virgin olive oil, divided

1 cup panko breadcrumbs

4 ounces pancetta, chopped

6 medium garlic cloves, minced

¼ cup tomato paste

½ teaspoon red pepper flakes

1½-pound head cauliflower, trimmed and cut into ½-inch pieces

8 ounces campanelle or orecchiette pasta

Kosher salt and ground black pepper

1 cup lightly packed fresh basil, chopped

Finely grated pecorino Romano cheese, to serve

In a large pot over medium, heat 2 tablespoons of oil until shimmering. Add the panko and cook, stirring occasionally, until golden brown, about 3 minutes; transfer to a small bowl.

In the same pot over medium, combine the remaining 2 tablespoons oil, the pancetta and garlic, then cook, stirring, until the garlic is lightly browned, about 2 minutes. Add the tomato paste and pepper flakes; cook, stirring, until the paste begins to brown, about 2 minutes. Pour in 4 cups water and scrape up any browned bits, then stir in the cauliflower, pasta and 1½ teaspoons salt. Bring to a simmer, then cover and cook, stirring occasionally, until the pasta is al dente and the cauliflower is tender, 10 to 12 minutes.

Off heat, taste and season with salt and pepper, then let stand for a few minutes to allow the pasta to absorb some of the sauce. Serve sprinkled with the panko, basil and pecorino.

Pearl Couscous Pilaf with Artichokes, Green Olives and Dill

Start to finish: 55 minutes (30 minutes active)
Servings: 4

Despite being cooked like a grain, pearl couscous, which also goes by the names Israeli couscous and ptitim, actually is a small, round pasta made from semolina. In this pilaf it gets a brief toast, bringing out sweet, nutty notes. We love the convenience of frozen artichoke hearts. Canned artichokes work, too; a 14-ounce can contains a little less than the amount called for here, but works fine. Pomegranate molasses, a thick syrup-like condiment made of concentrated pomegranate juice, provides sweet-tart notes that pair perfectly with warm allspice and briny olive. For added pops of color and fresh, tangy flavor, sprinkle a few tablespoons of pomegranate seeds over the dish just before serving.

1½ cups pearl couscous

4 tablespoons extra-virgin olive oil, divided

½ cup sliced almonds

1 large yellow onion, halved and thinly sliced

2 medium garlic cloves, thinly sliced

Kosher salt and ground black pepper

2 cups thawed frozen artichoke hearts, chopped (see headnote)

½ teaspoon ground allspice

½ cup pitted green olives, chopped

1 cup lightly packed fresh dill, chopped

2 teaspoons pomegranate molasses, plus more to serve

In a 12-inch skillet over medium-high, toast the couscous, stirring occasionally, until golden brown, 3 to 5 minutes. Transfer to a small bowl; set aside. In the same skillet over medium, add 2 tablespoons oil and the almonds. Cook, stirring often, until the almonds are golden brown, about 2 minutes. Transfer to another small bowl and set aside.

In the same skillet over medium-high, heat the remaining 2 tablespoons oil until shimmering. Add the onion, garlic and ½ teaspoon salt; cook, stirring occasionally, until golden brown, 5 to 8 minutes. Return the couscous to the skillet and add the artichokes, stirring to coat. Stir in 3 cups water, the allspice, 1½ teaspoons salt and 1 teaspoon pepper. Bring to a simmer, then cover, reduce to low and cook, undisturbed, until the couscous has absorbed most of the liquid, about 15 minutes.

Remove from the heat. Stir in the olives, half the dill and the pomegranate molasses. Taste and season with salt and pepper. Transfer to a serving dish and top with the toasted almonds, the remaining dill, an additional drizzle of pomegranate molasses and a sprinkle of black pepper.

Pasta with Broccolini, Anchovies and Garlic

Start to finish: 30 minutes
Servings: 4 to 6

This speedy one-pot pasta dish is a riff on classic orecchiette con cime di rapa, or orecchiette with broccoli rabe, from Puglia in southern Italy. We opt for sweet, mild Broccolini instead of broccoli rabe, which has a notable bitterness, and we cut the stalks into small pieces that combine well with the pasta. If you're a fan of rabe, feel free to use it, but reduce the cooking time by a minute or two, as rabe tenderizes more quickly. Oil-packed anchovies are sold in tins and jars that vary in size; a two-ounce container should contain about 12 fillets, the amount needed for this recipe.

1 pound campanelle, fusilli or other short pasta

Kosher salt and ground black pepper

¼ cup extra-virgin olive oil, plus more to serve

1 pound Broccolini, trimmed and cut into ½-inch pieces

12 oil-packed anchovy fillets (see headnote), finely chopped (about 2½ tablespoons)

5 medium garlic cloves, minced

½ to 1 teaspoon red pepper flakes

2 ounces pecorino Romano, finely grated (1 cup), plus more to serve

1 teaspoon grated lemon zest, plus 3 tablespoons lemon juice

In a large Dutch oven, bring 3 quarts water to a boil. Add the pasta and 2 teaspoons salt, then cook, stirring occasionally, until al dente. Reserve about 2 cups of the pasta cooking water, then drain in a colander; set aside.

In the same pot over medium-high, heat the oil until shimmering. Add the Broccolini and ¼ teaspoon salt; cook, stirring occasionally, until beginning to brown, 2 to 3 minutes. Add the anchovies, garlic and pepper flakes; cook, stirring, until fragrant, 1 to 2 minutes. Stir in 1 cup of the reserved pasta water, bring to a simmer and cook, stirring occasionally, until the Broccolini is tender, 5 to 7 minutes.

Stir the pasta into the Broccolini mixture and ½ cup pasta water. Remove from the heat and stir in ½ teaspoon black pepper and the cheese, followed by the lemon zest and juice; add more cooking water 1 tablespoon at a time as needed if the mixture looks dry. Taste and season with salt and black pepper. Serve drizzled with additional oil and sprinkled with additional cheese.

Orzo with Chicken, Tomatoes and Feta

Start to finish: 45 minutes
Servings: 4

The classic Greek stew known as giouvetsi (sometimes spelled youvetsi) is a comforting dish of tomatoes, spices, orzo and meat—often lamb or beef. To simplify preparation, our one-pot version calls for boneless, skinless chicken thighs. First we sear them on one side to develop a generous amount of browning, then we simmer the thighs along with the orzo in a warmly spiced tomato sauce seasoned with paprika, allspice and cinnamon.

1½ pounds boneless, skinless chicken thighs, trimmed

5 tablespoons extra-virgin olive oil, divided

4 tablespoons tomato paste, divided

1 teaspoon sweet paprika

¼ teaspoon plus ⅛ teaspoon ground allspice, divided

Kosher salt and ground black pepper

1 medium yellow onion, chopped

4 medium garlic cloves, minced

14½-ounce can whole peeled tomatoes, crushed by hand

3-inch cinnamon stick

1½ cups orzo

3 tablespoons fresh oregano, chopped

Crumbled feta cheese, to serve

In a medium bowl, toss together the chicken, 1 tablespoon oil, 1 tablespoon tomato paste, the paprika, ⅛ teaspoon allspice, and ½ teaspoon each salt and pepper.

In a Dutch oven over medium-high, heat 2 tablespoons of the remaining oil until shimmering. Add the chicken in an even layer, reserving the bowl; cook, without stirring, until browned on the bottom, about 2 minutes. Transfer to the reserved bowl; set aside.

In the same pot over medium-high, heat the remaining 2 tablespoons oil until shimmering. Add the onion and garlic; cook, stirring occasionally, until lightly browned, about 4 minutes. Add the remaining 3 tablespoons tomato paste and cook, stirring, until the paste begins to brown and stick to the pot, about 30 seconds. Add the tomatoes with juices, the cinnamon, remaining ¼ teaspoon allspice, ¾ teaspoon salt, ¼ teaspoon pepper and 5 cups water, then bring to a simmer.

Add the chicken and any accumulated juices, along with the orzo and oregano. Return to a simmer, then reduce to medium and cook, uncovered and stirring occasionally, until the orzo is tender and the chicken is cooked through, about 25 minutes. Off heat, remove and discard the cinnamon. Taste and season with salt and pepper. Serve sprinkled with feta.

"Orzotto" with Asparagus, Lemon and Parmesan

Start to finish: 30 minutes
Servings: 4

Traditionally made with medium-grain Italian rice, risotto gets its creaminess from a unique cooking method: adding liquid slowly and stirring vigorously to release the rice's starch. We've found that applying the technique to other "grains" yields a similarly rich, silky texture. So we cook orzo risotto-style in a 12-inch skillet to allow the broth to reduce quickly while providing plenty of room for stirring. The finished dish is a supple, velvety "orzotto." We love the combination of floral basil with grassy-sweet asparagus and tangy lemon, but parsley, dill or chives would be delicious as well.

2 tablespoons extra-virgin olive oil

1 medium shallot, minced

Kosher salt and ground black pepper

3 medium garlic cloves, peeled and thinly sliced

1 cup orzo

2 tablespoons dry white wine or vermouth

4 cups low-sodium chicken broth or vegetable broth, divided

1 pound asparagus, trimmed and cut into ½-inch pieces on the diagonal; stalks and tips reserved separately

1 teaspoon grated lemon zest, plus 2 tablespoons lemon juice

1 ounce finely grated Parmesan cheese (½ cup), plus more to serve

¼ cup lightly packed fresh basil, thinly sliced

In a 12-inch skillet over medium-high, heat the oil until shimmering. Add the shallot and ½ teaspoon salt; cook, stirring occasionally, until just beginning to soften, about 3 minutes. Add the garlic and cook, stirring, until fragrant, about 30 seconds. Stir in the orzo and cook, stirring often, until the shallot and garlic begin to brown, about 2 minutes.

Add the wine and cook, stirring, until fully evaporated. Stir in 2 cups broth and bring to a vigorous simmer. Cook, stirring often and briskly, making sure to scrape along the edges and sides of the pan, until the liquid is absorbed, about 5 minutes. Add 1 cup of the remaining broth and simmer vigorously, still stirring often and briskly, until the liquid is again absorbed, about 5 minutes.

Add the asparagus stalks and the remaining 1 cup broth; cook, stirring occasionally, until the asparagus is just shy of tender-crisp, about for 3 minutes. Add the asparagus tips and cook, stirring, until almost all the liquid has been absorbed and the asparagus is tender, another 2 minutes.

Off heat, stir in the lemon zest and juice, Parmesan and about half the basil. Taste and season with salt and pepper. Serve sprinkled with the remaining basil and additional Parmesan.

Maltese-Style Vermicelli Omelet

Start to finish: 45 minutes
Servings: 4

For this dish, our version of the Maltese vermicelli omelet called fraga tat tarja, the pasta does not need to be cooked before it's added to the skillet, making this a tidy one-pan recipe. In addition to pancetta for deep flavor, we've added wilted spinach instead of the more common sprinkling of parsley to give the omelet color and make it more a complete meal. A green salad dressed with lemon juice and olive oil is a nice accompaniment.

5 large eggs

1½ ounces pecorino Romano cheese, finely grated (¾ cup), plus more to serve

½ to ¾ teaspoon red pepper flakes

Kosher salt and ground black pepper

2 tablespoons extra-virgin olive oil

3 ounces thinly sliced pancetta, chopped

2 medium shallots, chopped

6 ounces vermicelli or capellini, broken in half

4 cups (3 ounces) lightly packed baby spinach

Heat the oven to 400°F with a rack in the middle position. In a medium bowl, whisk together the eggs, cheese, pepper flakes, 1 teaspoon salt and ½ teaspoon black pepper. In an oven-safe nonstick 12-inch skillet over medium, cook the 2 tablespoons oil and the pancetta, stirring occasionally, until the pancetta is golden brown, 3 to 5 minutes. Add the shallots and cook, stirring, until translucent, about 2 minutes.

Add 3 cups water and the vermicelli to the pan, then bring to a simmer. Cook, stirring, until the pasta has absorbed most of the liquid, about 7 minutes. Increase to medium-high, then stir in the spinach and cook until wilted, about 30 seconds. Pour in the egg mixture and stir to combine, then cook without stirring until the edges are browned, 5 to 7 minutes.

Transfer the pan to the oven and bake until the surface of the omelet is set, about 4 minutes. Remove from the oven (the handle will be hot) and run a silicone spatula around the edge and underneath the omelet to loosen, then slide it onto a cutting board. Cool for 5 minutes, then cut into wedges to serve. Serve sprinkled with additional cheese.

Harissa-Garlic Pearl Couscous and Shrimp

Start to finish: 35 minutes
Servings: 4

This recipe was inspired by Moroccan crevettes pil pil, a stewy, fragrant shrimp dish that is rich in fruity olive oil. The warm spices, smoky harissa, sweet-tart tomatoes and lots of garlic are a wonderful complement to plump, briny shrimp. Here, to round out the meal, we add pearl couscous. First, we toast the couscous in olive oil to enhance its nutty taste, then simmer it in the fragrant sauce. Be sure to use pearl couscous, also known as Israeli couscous or ptitim. A type of semolina pasta prized for its tender-chewy texture, it is more substantial than regular couscous.

1½ pounds extra-large (21/25 per pound) shrimp, peeled (tails removed), deveined and patted dry

1 teaspoon plus 1 tablespoon sweet paprika, divided

Kosher salt and ground black pepper

5 tablespoons extra-virgin olive oil, divided, plus more to serve

1½ cups pearl couscous

½ teaspoon caraway seeds, lightly crushed

6 medium garlic cloves, finely grated

2 tablespoons harissa paste, plus more to serve

8 ounces ripe tomatoes, cored and chopped, divided

1 tablespoon grated lemon zest, plus 2 tablespoons lemon juice

3 tablespoons finely chopped fresh cilantro

In a medium bowl, toss together the shrimp, the 1 teaspoon paprika and ½ teaspoon salt; set aside. In a 12-inch nonstick skillet over medium, heat 2 tablespoons of the oil until shimmering. Add the couscous and cook, stirring occasionally, until golden brown, 3 to 4 minutes. Transfer to a small bowl; set aside.

In the same skillet over medium, heat the remaining 3 tablespoons oil until shimmering. Add the caraway and cook, stirring, until fragrant, about 30 seconds. Add the garlic, harissa, the remaining 1 tablespoon paprika, ½ teaspoon salt and ¼ teaspoon pepper; cook, stirring, until fragrant, about 30 seconds. Add half of the tomatoes and cook, stirring, until warmed through, about 1 minute.

Add 3½ cups water and bring to a boil over high, then stir in the couscous. Reduce to medium and simmer, uncovered and stirring occasionally, until the couscous is tender and most of the liquid has been absorbed, about 13 minutes. Add the shrimp and cook, stirring occasionally, until opaque throughout, about 3 minutes.

Off heat, stir in the remaining tomatoes and the lemon zest and juice. Taste and season with salt and pepper. Serve sprinkled with the cilantro, drizzled with additional oil and with additional harissa on the side.

Fregola with Chicken, Chard and Sun-Dried Tomatoes

Start to finish: 35 minutes
Servings: 4

Fregola is a small, round pasta from Sardinia, an Italian island in the Mediterranean Sea. The pasta, a near relative of couscous, is made with semolina flour and water, but is oven toasted, giving it a nutty flavor and a resilient chewiness. This warming, stew-like recipe pairs fregola with tender chicken thighs and earthy chard. Sun-dried tomatoes provide an umami-rich backbone, while white wine adds light, crisp notes. If fregola is not available, pearl couscous is a decent stand-in, but it softens more quickly, so after adding the broth and bringing to a simmer, plan to cook for only six to eight minutes before adding the chard leaves.

¼ cup extra-virgin olive oil, plus more to serve

1 medium yellow onion, finely chopped

1 large carrot, peeled, quartered lengthwise and cut into ¼-inch pieces

1 small bunch rainbow Swiss chard, stems thinly sliced, leaves roughly chopped, reserved separately

6 medium garlic cloves, minced

Kosher salt and ground black pepper

1 cup fregola (see headnote)

¼ cup drained oil-packed sun-dried tomatoes, finely chopped

1 pound boneless, skinless chicken thighs, trimmed and cut into 1-inch pieces

1 cup dry white wine

1 quart low-sodium chicken broth

1 rosemary sprig

In a large pot over medium, heat the oil until shimmering. Add the onion, carrot, chard stems, garlic and ½ teaspoon salt. Cook, stirring occasionally, until the vegetables are softened, 4 to 5 minutes. Add the fregola and sun-dried tomatoes, stirring to combine, followed by the chicken. Add the wine, increase to medium-high and cook, stirring, until mostly evaporated, 2 to 3 minutes.

Stir in the broth and rosemary, then bring to a simmer. Reduce to medium and simmer, uncovered and stirring occasionally, until most of the liquid has been absorbed and the fregola is just shy of tender, 20 to 25 minutes.

Add the chard leaves and cook, stirring often, until the fregola and chard leaves are tender and the mixture is creamy but not soupy, about 5 minutes. Off heat, remove and discard the rosemary, then taste and season with salt and pepper. Serve drizzled with additional oil.

One-Pot Pasta all'Arrabbiata

Start to finish: 20 minutes
Servings: 4 to 6

Pasta all'arrabbiata, from the Lazio region of Italy, features a spicy marriage of tomatoes, garlic and pepper flakes (arrabbiata translates as "angry"). This one-pot version cooks the pasta directly in the sauce, so there's no need to dirty two pots and heat up the kitchen. We like this made with enough pepper flakes for moderate but not overly assertive heat; adjust the amount to suit your taste. We call for Parmesan cheese, but pecorino Romano also is good. We like to garnish the pasta with fresh basil.

3 tablespoons extra-virgin olive oil, plus more to serve

4 medium garlic cloves, thinly sliced

½ teaspoon red pepper flakes

14½-ounce can diced tomatoes

Kosher salt and ground black pepper

1 pound penne pasta

1 ounce finely grated Parmesan (½ cup), plus more to serve

In a large pot, combine the oil, garlic and pepper flakes. Cook over medium-high, stirring often, until fragrant, about 1 minute. Add the tomatoes with juices, 1 teaspoon salt and ½ teaspoon black pepper. Add 3 cups water and the pasta; stir to combine. Bring to a boil over medium-high, then reduce to medium, cover and cook, stirring occasionally, until the pasta is al dente, 9 to 11 minutes.

Remove the pot from the heat and stir in the cheese. Cover and let stand for 5 minutes. Stir vigorously, then taste and season with salt and black pepper. Serve drizzled with additional oil and sprinkled with additional cheese.

Spaghetti with Goat Cheese, Mint and Peas

Start to finish: 25 minutes
Servings: 4

In this one-pot pasta dish, our simplified take on a recipe from "Rich Table" by Evan and Sarah Rich, the full, fresh flavors belie the ultra-easy preparation. The sauce requires no cooking and the only knife work is chopping the mint. Make sure to fully thaw the peas so the ½ cup for mashing break down easily. Have the goat cheese at room temperature, too, so it becomes soft and creamy when mixed into the mashed peas.

12 ounces spaghetti

Kosher salt and ground black pepper

1 cup frozen peas, thawed, divided

4 ounces fresh goat cheese (chèvre), room temperature

1 teaspoon grated lime zest, plus 1 tablespoon lime juice

⅓ cup extra-virgin olive oil

½ cup chopped fresh mint

In a large pot, bring 4 quarts of water to a boil. Stir in the pasta and 1 tablespoon salt, then cook, stirring occasionally, until al dente. Reserve about 1 cup of the cooking water, then drain the pasta and return it to the pot.

Meanwhile, in a medium bowl, use a fork to mash ½ cup of the peas to a coarse puree. Add the goat cheese, lime zest and juice, oil, half of the mint, ¼ teaspoon salt and ¾ teaspoon pepper. Continue to mash until well combined; set aside.

To the drained pasta in the pot, add the goat cheese mixture, the remaining peas and ¾ cup of the reserved cooking water. Toss until evenly coated, adding more cooking water 1 tablespoon at a time as needed so the sauce is creamy and clings to the pasta. Taste and season with salt and pepper. Serve sprinkled with the remaining mint.

Korean Chicken and Noodle Stew with Potatoes and Mushrooms

Start to finish: 40 minutes
Servings: 4 to 6

Inspired by jjimdak, a Korean chicken and vegetable stew, this flavor-packed dish gets a hit of heat from gochujang, plus umami from mushrooms and soy sauce. The noodles become translucent, with a pleasantly chewy and springy texture, and absorb the flavors around them. You can find dang myun in most Asian markets or order them online. If they're unavailable, cellophane noodles, also known as bean threads, are a good alternative; soak them and add them just as you would dang myun. We like this topped with either toasted sesame oil or toasted sesame seeds.

¼ cup soy sauce

2 tablespoons mirin

2 tablespoons gochujang

2 tablespoons packed brown sugar

1 pound boneless, skinless chicken thighs, trimmed and cut into ½-inch pieces

8 ounces shiitake mushrooms, stemmed, caps thinly sliced

8 ounces Yukon Gold potatoes, peeled and cut into ½-inch cubes

1 bunch scallions, white parts thinly sliced, green parts cut into 1-inch lengths, reserved separately

3 medium cloves garlic, minced

Kosher salt and ground black pepper

6 ounces sweet potato noodles (dang myun; see headnote)

Boiling water, for soaking the noodles

In a large Dutch oven over medium, combine the soy sauce, mirin, gochujang and sugar. Add the chicken, mushrooms, potatoes, scallion whites, garlic, ½ teaspoon salt and ¼ teaspoon pepper. Stir, then add 3 cups water. Bring to a gentle boil over high, then cover, reduce to medium and simmer, stirring occasionally, until the potatoes are tender and the chicken is cooked through, 10 to 15 minutes.

Meanwhile, place the noodles in a large heatproof bowl and add boiling water to cover. Let stand, stirring once or twice, until the noodles are pliable, 5 to 10 minutes, then drain. If the noodles are in very long strands, snip them with kitchen shears in several places to cut them into shorter lengths.

Stir the noodles and scallion greens into the stew. Cook, uncovered and stirring occasionally, until the noodles are tender but still springy and the scallion greens have wilted, about 3 minutes.

Pasta with Tomato, Onion and Butter

Start to finish: 35 minutes
Servings: 4 to 6

Marcella Hazan's famous tomato sauce with onion and butter, from her book "The Essentials of Classic Italian Cooking," transforms three simple ingredients into a luscious sauce. Our pantry-focused version replaces the fresh tomatoes with a can of tomato paste to create a dish that can be on the table in minutes. To enhance the sweetness and umami, we finish the sauce with a splash of balsamic vinegar (white balsamic also is great) and nutty Parmesan cheese. If you don't have spaghetti, use another type of pasta, such as fettuccine or linguine. Fresh basil is a great addition; if you have it on hand, toss some into the pasta just before serving.

1 pound spaghetti

Kosher salt and ground black pepper

4 tablespoons salted butter, cut into 1-tablespoon pieces, divided

1 small yellow onion, chopped

6-ounce can tomato paste

1 tablespoon balsamic vinegar

1 ounce Parmesan cheese, finely grated (½ cup), plus more to serve

In a large pot, bring 4 quarts water to a boil. Add the pasta and 1 tablespoon salt, then cook, stirring occasionally, until al dente. Reserve 2 cups of the cooking water, then drain; set aside.

In the same pot over medium, melt 2 tablespoons butter. Add the onion, reduce to low, cover and cook, stirring occasionally, until the onion has softened, 12 to 14 minutes.

Add the tomato paste, ½ teaspoon pepper and 1½ cups of the reserved cooking water, then whisk until smooth. Add the pasta, the remaining 2 tablespoons butter and the vinegar. Using tongs, toss until the sauce clings to the pasta, the pasta is heated through and the butter is melted, adding more cooking water if needed so the noodles are lightly sauced.

Off heat, toss in the Parmesan, then taste and season with salt and pepper. Serve sprinkled with additional Parmesan.

Catalan Noodles with Pork and Chorizo

Start to finish: 50 minutes
Servings: 4 to 6

Known as fideos a la cazuela, this one-pan noodle dish from Catalonia, in northeastern Spain, takes its name from the wide, shallow earthenware pan, or cazuela, in which it traditionally is cooked. The comforting dish typically features pork, chicken or other meat; we opt for pork shoulder plus cured Spanish chorizo, which contributes rich, smoky flavor. In place of the fideos—short, thin noodles that are typically toasted—we use elbow macaroni. Peas and fresh parsley add pops of color. Some recipes season the cazuela with picada, the Catalan mixture of nuts, bread, garlic and other aromatics pounded or ground to a thick paste. To streamline prep, we garnish the finished casserole with some of those same ingredients.

2 tablespoons extra-virgin olive oil, divided, plus more to serve

1 pound boneless pork shoulder, trimmed and cut into ½-inch chunks

4 ounces Spanish chorizo, halved lengthwise, then cut crosswise into ¼-inch half moons

Kosher salt and ground black pepper

¼ cup slivered almonds

14½-ounce can diced tomatoes

1 medium yellow onion, finely chopped

2 medium garlic cloves, minced

½ cup dry white wine

8 ounces medium elbow macaroni

1 cup frozen peas, thawed

¾ cup chopped fresh flat-leaf parsley

In a 12-inch skillet over medium, heat 1 tablespoon oil until shimmering. Add the pork, chorizo and ½ teaspoon each salt and pepper. Cook, stirring occasionally, until the chorizo is browned all over, about 8 minutes. Using a slotted spoon, transfer the meat to a plate; set aside.

In the same skillet over medium, add the almonds and the remaining 1 tablespoon oil. Cook, stirring, until lightly toasted, 1 to 2 minutes. Using a slotted spoon, transfer to a paper towel-lined plate; set aside.

To the same skillet over medium, add the tomatoes with juices, onion and garlic, followed by the meat and any accumulated juices. Cook, scraping up any browned bits and stirring occasionally, until the onion is soft and the sauce has thickened, about 10 minutes. Add the wine and cook, stirring occasionally, until the liquid has evaporated, about 3 minutes.

Stir in the pasta and 3 cups water, then bring to a simmer over medium-high. Reduce to medium and cook, uncovered and stirring occasionally, until the pasta is al dente, about 10 minutes. Add the peas and cook, stirring occasionally, until heated through, about 2 minutes.

Off heat, stir in half the parsley, then taste and season with salt and pepper. Serve sprinkled with the almonds and the remaining parsley and drizzled with additional oil.

Crispy Pasta with Chickpeas, Lemon and Parsley

Start to finish: 35 minutes
Servings: 4

This unusual dish from the Puglia region of Italy combines pieces of crisp fried pasta, al dente boiled pasta and tender chickpeas. We learned it from Anna Carmela Perrone at Le Zie Trattoria in Lecce. We use a 9-ounce package of fresh fettuccine and cut the noodles into 2-inch lengths; half is toasted in olive oil and the other half is simmered directly in the sauce. If you have trouble finding fresh pasta, use an 8.8-ounce package of dried pappardelle made with egg; the noodles are packaged in nests that are easy to break into pieces. Keep in mind, however, that dried pappardelle toasts more quickly than fresh pasta—in about 8 minutes. Lemon zest and juice and chopped fresh parsley add brightness to balance the starches. This dish is best served right away when the sauce is creamy.

¼ cup extra-virgin olive oil

9 ounces fresh fettuccine, cut into rough 2-inch lengths

15½-ounce can chickpeas, drained, liquid reserved

2 bay leaves

Kosher salt and ground black pepper

2 teaspoons grated lemon zest, plus 1 teaspoon lemon juice

½ cup lightly packed fresh flat-leaf parsley, chopped

In a large pot over medium, combine the oil and half of the pasta. Cook, stirring occasionally, until the pasta is crisp and deeply browned, 12 to 14 minutes. Using a slotted spoon, transfer to a medium bowl and set aside.

To the oil remaining in the pot, add the chickpeas and bay. Cook, stirring occasionally, until the chickpeas darken slightly and the bay is toasted, 2 to 4 minutes. Stir in the remaining pasta, ¾ cup of chickpea liquid (supplement with water if needed), 2¼ cups water, 1 teaspoon salt and ¾ teaspoon pepper. Bring to a simmer over medium-high and cook, stirring occasionally, until the pasta is heated through and slightly softened, about 2 minutes.

Add the toasted pasta and cook, stirring often and adjusting the heat as needed to maintain a gentle simmer, until the untoasted pasta is al dente and the sauce lightly clings, about 4 minutes. Remove the pot from the heat, then remove and discard the bay. Stir in the lemon zest and juice and parsley. Taste and season with salt and pepper.

Pasta and Seafood "Paella"

Start to finish: 45 minutes
Servings: 6 to 8

A close relative of paella, fideuà includes short noodles instead of rice. But like paella, it features a variety of fresh seafood. The one-pot dish originated in Valencia, on Spain's southeastern coast, but today often is associated with Catalonia, in the northeastern part of the country. It typically is made with short, thin noodles known as fideos, though capellini or vermicelli pasta, broken into 2-inch lengths, works equally well. First they're tossed with olive oil and toasted to impart a deep, nutty taste. The noodles then are cooked along with the seafood so they absorb the flavorful broth, which we season with smoked paprika.

6 tablespoons extra-virgin olive oil, divided

6 ounces capellini or vermicelli, broken into rough 2-inch pieces

8 ounces skinless cod, snapper, halibut or monkfish fillets, about 1 inch thick, cut into 1-inch chunks

6 ounces extra-large (21/25 per pound) shrimp, peeled (tails removed), deveined

Kosher salt and ground black pepper

1 medium yellow onion, halved and cut into 1-inch pieces

1 medium red bell pepper, stemmed, seeded and cut into 1-inch pieces

1 pint grape or cherry tomatoes, halved

6 medium garlic cloves, minced

2½ teaspoons smoked paprika

½ cup dry white wine

8 ounces mussels, scrubbed and debearded

¼ cup finely chopped fresh flat-leaf parsley

Lemon wedges, to serve

Aioli, to serve

Heat the oven to 350°F with a rack in the middle position. In a 12-inch oven-safe skillet, stir together 3 tablespoons oil and the pasta. Cook, tossing often with tongs, until the pasta is golden brown, about 6 minutes. Transfer to a plate and set aside; reserve the skillet. In a medium bowl, toss together the cod, shrimp, ¼ teaspoon salt and ⅛ teaspoon pepper; set aside.

In the same skillet over medium-high, heat the remaining 3 tablespoons oil until shimmering. Add the onion, bell pepper, ¾ teaspoon salt and ¼ teaspoon pepper; cook, stirring occasionally, until softened, 5 to 6 minutes.

Add the tomatoes, garlic and paprika; cook, stirring, until the tomatoes begin to soften, 1 to 2 minutes. Add the wine and cook, scraping up any browned bits, until the liquid is slightly reduced, 1 to 2 minutes. Add 2 cups water and bring to a simmer. Add the pasta and cook, uncovered and stirring occasionally, until the liquid has reduced by more than half, 5 to 6 minutes.

Off heat, nestle the cod, shrimp and mussels into the noodles. Place in the oven and bake until the noodles are tender, the cod and shrimp are opaque throughout and the mussels have opened, about 8 minutes; discard any mussels that have not opened. Sprinkle with parsley and serve with lemon wedges and aioli.

Aioli

Start to finish: 5 minutes
Makes about ¾ cup

In a small bowl, stir together **2 medium garlic cloves** (finely grated) and **2 tablespoons lemon juice** or **sherry vinegar;** let stand for 5 minutes. Whisk in **½ cup mayonnaise, 2 tablespoons extra-virgin olive oil** and **¼ teaspoon kosher salt.** Just before serving, taste and season with kosher salt and ground black pepper.

Hearty Pastas

Spaetzle with Sage, Ham and Gouda

In a 12-inch nonstick skillet over medium, heat **3 tablespoons extra-virgin olive oil** until shimmering. Add **¼ cup lightly packed fresh whole sage, 3 medium garlic cloves** (smashed and peeled), and cook, stirring, until the sage is lightly crisped and fragrant, about 2 minutes. Off heat, use a slotted spoon to transfer the sage to a small plate; remove and discard the garlic. Return the skillet to medium and stir in **2 ounces thinly sliced smoked deli ham** (chopped), **½ teaspoon red pepper flakes** and **1 recipe Spaetzle.** Cook, stirring occasionally, until the Spaetzle is heated through and lightly browned, about 5 minutes. Crumble the sage into the skillet and stir to combine. Off heat, add **2 tablespoons salted butter** (cut into 2 pieces) and stir until melted. Taste and season with **kosher salt** and **ground black pepper.** Transfer to a serving dish and sprinkle with ¼ cup finely shredded **Gouda cheese.**

Spaetzle

Start to finish: 1 hour (30 minutes active)
Servings: 4

Spaetzle, which means "little sparrows" in German, are small, rustic dumplings—some call them noodles—made from a simple batter of flour, eggs and milk or water. The dumplings are formed by dropping the batter through the perforations of a Spaetzle maker, which resembles a large-holed cheese grater, into boiling water. Scooped from the water or drained, the cooked Spaetzle are unevenly shaped and charming, with a toothsome texture and agreeable flavor that makes them an excellent accompaniment to stews and braises. They can also be sautéed in butter and embellished with other ingredients, such as herbs and cheese. Spaetzle makers are relatively inexpensive and easy to source, but if not an option, you can improvise with a flat cheese grater with holes the size of the large holes on a box grater. Hold the grater above the boiling water, ladle on some batter and use a silicone spatula to work the batter back and forth and push it through the holes.

2 cups all-purpose flour	1 cup whole milk
¼ teaspoon freshly grated nutmeg	2 large whole eggs
Kosher salt and ground black pepper	

In a large bowl, whisk together the flour, nutmeg, 1 teaspoon salt and ½ teaspoon pepper. In a medium bowl, whisk together the milk and eggs. Gradually whisk the milk mixture into the flour mixture until a smooth batter forms; do not overmix. Cover with plastic wrap and let rest at room temperature for 30 minutes.

Line a rimmed baking sheet with kitchen parchment. In a large Dutch oven, bring 4 quarts water to a boil. Stir in 1 tablespoon salt. Set a Spaetzle maker over the pot. Scrape about half of the batter into the hopper of the Spaetzle maker and, working quickly, move the hopper back and forth until all of the batter has dropped into the boiling water. Return the water to a boil and cook for 1 minute, stirring once or twice; the Spaetzle will float to the surface after about 30 seconds, before they are cooked through.

Using a slotted spoon, transfer the Spaetzle to a colander set in a bowl. Rinse, tossing, under cold water until cool to the touch. Drain well, shaking the colander to remove as much water as possible, then distribute in an even layer on the prepared baking sheet. Cook the remaining batter in the same way, then rinse, drain and distribute on the baking sheet with the first batch. Use right away or cover with plastic wrap and refrigerate up to 2 days; bring to room temperature before finishing.

Buttered Spaetzle with Paprika and Herbs

In a 12-inch nonstick skillet over medium, melt **2 tablespoons salted butter.** Stir in **½ teaspoon sweet paprika,** then add **1 recipe Spaetzle;** cook, uncovered and stirring occasionally, until heated through and lightly browned, about 5 minutes. Off heat, stir in **3 tablespoons finely chopped fresh chives** and **3 tablespoons finely chopped fresh dill.** Taste and season with **kosher salt** and **ground black pepper.**

North African Chicken Couscous

Start to finish: 1¼ hours (40 minutes active)
Servings: 6

We got an education in couscous in Tunisia, including a lesson from Amel Cherif, a home cook who showed us the basics of making light, flavorful couscous. For our version, we use an 8-quart pot fitted with a stackable steamer insert that sits on top. If you don't own one, a large pot and a folding steamer basket worked well, too. Whisking the liquid from the stew into the steamed couscous is a key step, deeply flavoring the grain-like pasta and helping it stay fluffy and distinct. Harissa is a North African chili and spice paste that adds heat and complex flavor. If you can find DEA brand, sold in a tube and cans, it's our preferred harissa. We start the recipe using ¼ cup harissa to flavor the stew, then finish by mixing another ¼ cup into the stew liquid just before whisking it with the steamed couscous. If your harissa is particularly spicy or you prefer less heat, reduce the second addition of harissa.

2 cups couscous

4 tablespoons extra-virgin olive oil, divided, plus more to serve

Kosher salt and ground black pepper

1½ tablespoons ground turmeric

2 pounds boneless, skinless chicken thighs, trimmed and halved crosswise

1 pound Yukon Gold potatoes, cut into 1½-inch chunks

6 medium carrots, peeled, halved lengthwise and cut into 2-inch pieces

1 large red onion, root end intact, peeled and cut into 8 wedges

2 jalapeño chilies, stemmed and thinly sliced

6 medium garlic cloves, minced

2 tablespoons tomato paste

½ cup harissa paste (more or less, to taste), divided

Lemon wedges, to serve

In a medium bowl, combine the couscous and 2 tablespoons oil, rubbing with your fingers until coated. Stir in 1¼ cups water and ¼ teaspoon salt; let stand for 15 minutes.

Meanwhile, in a medium bowl, stir together the turmeric, ½ teaspoon salt and 1 teaspoon pepper. Add the chicken and toss to coat; set aside for 15 minutes. In a large bowl, combine the potatoes, carrots, onion, 1 tablespoon of the remaining oil, ½ teaspoon salt and 1 teaspoon pepper. Toss to coat, then set aside.

Stir the couscous to separate the granules, then mound it in a steamer insert or basket that fits into an 8-quart pot; set aside. Set the 8-quart pot over medium-high and heat the remaining 1 tablespoon oil until barely smoking. Add the jalapeños and cook, stirring occasionally, until slightly softened, about 1 minute. Add the garlic, tomato paste and ¼ cup harissa; cook, stirring, until the mixture begins to brown, 1 to 2 minutes.

Add 2 cups water and bring to a simmer. Place the chicken in the pot, then top with the vegetables and any liquid in the bowl; do not stir. Bring to a simmer, then set the steamer insert or basket with the couscous on the pot; if using a folding steamer basket, set it directly on the vegetables. Cover, reduce to low and cook, maintaining a gentle simmer, until the chicken and vegetables are tender, about 45 minutes; do not stir the couscous or the stew.

Remove the steamer basket and transfer the couscous to a large bowl; cover with foil to keep warm. Stir the vegetables into the chicken, cover and let stand for 5 minutes.

Using a slotted spoon, transfer the chicken and vegetables to a large bowl; taste and season with salt and pepper. Measure out 2 cups of the cooking liquid in the pot. Stir the remaining ¼ cup harissa into it.

Whisk the couscous until no clumps remain, then whisk in the cooking liquid-harissa mixture. Taste and season with salt and pepper. Transfer the couscous to a large, deep platter and make a well at the center. Spoon the chicken and vegetables into the well. Drizzle with additional oil and serve with lemon wedges.

Noodle Kugel with Leeks, Mushrooms and Goat Cheese

Start to finish: 1 hour 10 minutes (25 minutes active), plus cooling
Servings: 6 to 8

A traditional Ashkenazi Jewish casserole with deep roots in Eastern Europe, a kugel is made with noodles or sometimes potatoes. It's also called lokshen kugel, which means "noodle pudding" in Yiddish. The dish can be sweet or savory, and the variations of add-ins and toppings are endless. Often enriched with dairy products like cream cheese, cottage cheese and sour cream, kugel is popular at gatherings during the Jewish holiday of Shavuot, after Passover. We've created a savory version featuring tender sautéed mushrooms and leeks—it's delicious as a main dish or a side. We add goat cheese to the eggs and sour cream to impart a pleasant tanginess, then bake the kugel until golden brown, producing an appealing crisped-noodle surface.

1 tablespoon salted butter, room temperature, plus 3 tablespoons salted butter, cut into 3 pieces

2 large leeks, white and light green parts thinly sliced, rinsed, drained and patted dry

8 ounces cremini mushrooms or a mixture of cremini, oyster and stemmed shiitake mushrooms, trimmed and thinly sliced

½ cup lightly packed fresh flat-leaf parsley, chopped

2 tablespoons fresh thyme, finely chopped

Kosher salt and ground black pepper

12 ounces wide egg noodles

6 large eggs

2 cups sour cream

1 cup low-sodium vegetable or mushroom broth

4 ounces fresh goat cheese (chèvre), room temperature

Heat the oven to 350°F with a rack in the middle position. Coat a 9-by-13-inch baking dish with the 1 tablespoon room-temperature butter.

In a 12-inch skillet over medium, melt the remaining 3 tablespoons butter. Add the leeks, mushrooms, parsley, thyme and ½ teaspoon salt. Cook, stirring occasionally, until the leeks and mushrooms are softened and lightly browned, 8 to 10 minutes. Remove the pan from the heat and let cool.

Meanwhile, in a large pot, bring 4 quarts water to a boil. Add the noodles and 1 tablespoon salt, then cook, stirring occasionally, until just shy of al dente. Drain in a colander, then let cool until warm to the touch, about 10 minutes.

While the noodles cool, in a large bowl, whisk together the eggs, sour cream, broth, goat cheese, ½ teaspoon salt and 1 teaspoon pepper until smooth; set aside. Add the leek-mushroom mixture and the noodles to the bowl with the egg mixture and stir. Pour the mixture into the prepared baking dish, distributing the noodles evenly.

Bake until the kugel is golden brown on top, does not jiggle at the center when the dish is gently shaken and registers 160°F at the center, 40 to 45 minutes. Transfer to a wire rack and cool for about 10 minutes. Serve warm.

Spaghetti and Meatballs

Start to finish: 1½ hours
Servings: 4 to 6

Spaghetti and meatballs each are popular foods in Italy, but the two are never served together as they are in all-American "spaghetti and meatballs." Nevertheless, we took the lessons we learned in Naples on how to make polpette Napoletane—Neapolitan meatballs that are ultra-tender and generously sized—and created this family-friendly comfort food classic. We brown the meatballs in the oven rather than fry them on the stovetop so there's less splatter, then a 20-minute simmer in the sauce gives the flavors a chance to deepen and meld.

2 tablespoons extra-virgin olive oil, plus more to serve

1 medium yellow onion, finely chopped

Kosher salt and ground black pepper

4 medium garlic cloves, finely grated

1 teaspoon red pepper flakes, divided

½ cup panko breadcrumbs

2 ounces pecorino Romano cheese, finely grated (1 cup), plus more to serve

1 large egg

½ cup finely chopped fresh flat-leaf parsley

1 pound 80 percent lean ground beef

28-ounce can crushed tomatoes

6 to 8 large fresh basil leaves, plus ¼ cup finely chopped

1 teaspoon white sugar

1 pound spaghetti

Heat the oven to 450°F with a rack in the middle position. Line a rimmed baking sheet with kitchen parchment. In a large Dutch oven over medium-high, heat the oil until shimmering. Add the onion and ¼ teaspoon salt; cook, stirring occasionally, until softened, about 5 minutes. Add the garlic and ½ teaspoon pepper flakes; cook, stirring, until fragrant, about 30 seconds. Remove from the heat. Transfer half the onion mixture to a large bowl and cool until barely warm, about 20 minutes; leave the remaining onion mixture in the pot.

To the onion mixture in the bowl, add the panko and ½ cup water; press the panko into the water and let stand until the panko absorbs the liquid, about 5 minutes. Using a fork, mix well. Stir in the pecorino, egg, parsley, ½ teaspoon salt and 1 teaspoon black pepper. Add the beef and mix with your hands until homogeneous.

Using a ¼-cup dry measuring cup, portion the mixture onto the prepared baking sheet; you should have about 12 portions. Using your hands, shape each into a ball and return to the baking sheet. (If the mixture is sticky, lightly moisten your hands with water.) Bake until lightly browned, about 15 minutes. Remove from the oven.

While the meatballs bake, to the Dutch oven, add the tomatoes, basil leaves, sugar, the remaining ½ teaspoon pepper flakes and 1 cup water. Bring to a simmer over medium and cook, uncovered and stirring occasionally, until slightly thickened, about 15 minutes. Taste and season with salt and black pepper.

Using a large spoon, transfer the meatballs to the sauce, turning each to coat. Bring to a gentle simmer over medium, then reduce to medium-low, cover and cook for 20 minutes, stirring occasionally.

Meanwhile, in a large pot, bring 4 quarts of water to a boil. Stir in 1 tablespoon salt and the spaghetti, then cook, stirring occasionally, until just shy of al dente. Reserve about ½ cup of the cooking water, then drain.

Using a slotted spoon, transfer the meatballs to a large plate. Stir the chopped basil into the sauce, then add the spaghetti and ¼ cup of the reserved cooking water. Cook over medium, stirring, until the spaghetti is al dente, 2 to 3 minutes; add more cooking water 1 tablespoon at a time as needed if the mixture looks dry. Taste and season with salt and pepper. Transfer the spaghetti and sauce to a serving dish or individual bowls and top with the meatballs. Drizzle with additional oil and serve sprinkled with additional cheese.

Whole-Wheat Pasta with Chard, Potatoes and Fontina

Start to finish: 50 minutes
Servings: 6 to 8

Pizzoccheri is a regional specialty of Lombardy, in northern Italy, that pairs buckwheat pasta with cabbage, potatoes, melty mountain cheese and an abundance of butter. It inspired this recipe, but we use leafy-green Swiss chard, a generous dose of fresh sage and both lemon zest and juice, creating a one-pot wonder that is lighter and fresher than pizzoccheri yet still hearty and autumnal. We also think it's one of the best uses of whole-wheat pasta. When prepping the chard, thinly slice the stems and cut the leaves crosswise into thin ribbons. The greens are added to the pasta partway through cooking and the stems are sautéed in butter with the aromatics, so make sure to reserve them separately. If you have them, we also like to add 1 tablespoon caraway seeds, lightly crushed, along with the garlic and sage.

1 pound Yukon Gold potatoes, peeled and cut into ½-inch cubes

Kosher salt and ground black pepper

1 pound whole-wheat linguine or fettuccine, broken into 2-inch lengths

1 large bunch (about 1 pound) Swiss chard, stems thinly sliced, leaves sliced crosswise about ½ inch thick, reserved separately

6 tablespoons salted butter, cut into 1-tablespoon pieces

¼ cup thinly sliced fresh sage

4 medium garlic cloves, thinly sliced

1 teaspoon grated lemon zest, plus 3 tablespoons lemon juice

8 ounces fontina or Gruyère cheese, shredded (2 cups)

2 ounces Parmesan cheese, finely grated (1 cup), divided

In a large Dutch oven over medium-high, combine 4 quarts water, the potatoes and 1 tablespoon salt. Bring to a simmer and cook, uncovered and stirring once or twice, until tender, 4 to 6 minutes. Using a slotted spoon, transfer the potatoes to a bowl; set aside. Return the water to a boil and add the pasta. Cook, stirring occasionally, for 5 minutes. Stir in the chard leaves and cook, stirring occasionally, until the pasta is al dente and the chard is tender, another 5 minutes. Reserve about 2 cups of the cooking water, then drain in a colander and set aside.

In the same pot over medium, melt the butter. Cook, stirring occasionally, until golden brown with a nutty aroma, about 3 minutes. Add the chard stems, sage and garlic; cook, stirring occasionally, until fragrant and the chard stems begin to soften, 3 to 5 minutes.

Reduce to medium-low and stir in the potatoes, the pasta-chard mixture, lemon zest and juice and 1½ cups reserved cooking water. Stir in the fontina and half of the Parmesan. Cook, stirring, until the cheese is melted and the mixture is silky, 3 to 4 minutes; stir in more reserved pasta cooking water as needed to thin. Taste and season with salt and pepper. Serve sprinkled with the remaining Parmesan.

Tuna and Pasta Gratin

Start to finish: 50 minutes, plus cooling
Servings: 6 to 8

Our update to tuna noodle casserole incorporates a few fresh, grown-up changes, transforming the dish into a fantastic meal-in-one with lots of pleasing textural contrast. Anise-y fennel and soft, sweet sautéed onions build a flavor foundation, with white wine for hits of bright acidity. The mixture is combined with cream, plus earthy thyme and briny capers before being tossed with shell pasta and nutty Gruyère cheese. An herbed crouton topping, made extra-crisp by a quick bake, brings crunch to each bite. Either olive oil- or water-packed tuna works here; we prefer the former, as its flavor and texture are richer.

4 tablespoons salted butter, cut into 1-tablespoon pieces, divided

2 tablespoons extra-virgin olive oil, divided

6 ounces country-style white bread, crusts removed, torn into bite-size pieces (about 3 cups)

3 tablespoons fresh thyme, divided, plus more to serve

Kosher salt and ground black pepper

1 pound shell pasta

2 medium yellow onions, halved and thinly sliced

2 medium fennel bulbs, trimmed and finely chopped, fronds torn into bite-size pieces and reserved separately

½ cup dry white wine

1½ cups heavy cream

¼ cup drained capers

8 ounces Gruyère cheese, shredded (2 cups), divided

Two 5-ounce cans tuna, preferably packed in olive oil (see headnote), drained and flaked

Heat the oven to 400°F with a rack in the middle position. In a large Dutch oven over medium, heat 1 tablespoon each butter and oil until the butter melts. Add the bread, 1 tablespoon thyme and ¼ teaspoon each salt and pepper. Stir until the bread has absorbed the fat, about 1 minute. Transfer to a large plate and set aside. Wipe out the pot.

In the same pot over high, bring 3 quarts water to a boil. Add 1 tablespoon salt and the pasta; cook, stirring occasionally, until just shy of al dente. Reserve ½ cup cooking water, then drain; set aside.

Return the pot to medium and heat the remaining 3 tablespoons butter and the remaining 1 tablespoon oil until the butter melts. Add the onions, fennel, ½ teaspoon salt and ¼ teaspoon pepper. Cover and cook, stirring occasionally, until softened and beginning to brown, 10 to 12 minutes.

Add the wine and cook, scraping up any browned bits, until most of the liquid has evaporated, about 3 minutes. Stir in the cream and bring to a simmer. Stir in the capers and 2 tablespoons thyme. Add the pasta and the reserved pasta water, tossing until well combined. Remove from the heat.

Set aside ¼ cup of the Gruyère for sprinkling, then add the remaining 1¾ cups cheese to the pasta mixture along with the tuna; fold to combine. Taste and season with salt and pepper. Transfer the mixture to a 9-by-13-inch baking dish and distribute in an even layer. Top evenly with the bread mixture, then sprinkle with the remaining cheese. Bake until golden brown and the cheese is melted, 10 to 15 minutes. Sprinkle with additional thyme and fennel fronds. Cool for 10 minutes, then serve.

Udon Noodles with Spicy Meat and Mushroom Sauce

Start to finish: 50 minutes
Servings: 6

Thick, hearty homemade udon noodles are a perfect match for a meaty, umami-rich sauce. This delicious pairing comes from "Japanese Home Cooking" by Sonoko Sakai, Los Angeles-based cookbook author and cooking instructor. If you wish to use store-bought dried udon, 12 ounces is a good amount; boil the noodles in plenty of water until tender, then drain and rinse them as directed in the recipe. A salty fermented chili-bean paste called toban djan provides the spiciness; use the smaller dose if you're sensitive to chili heat. If you've used the larger amount and still want more heat in the sauced noodles, offer a bottle of chili oil at the table.

1 recipe (about 1¾ pounds) homemade udon noodles (see recipe p. 5), cooked, drained and rinsed (see headnote)

½ English cucumber

2 tablespoons cornstarch

2 tablespoons toasted sesame oil

8 ounces 80 percent lean ground beef

8 ounces ground pork

4 shiitake mushrooms, stemmed, caps finely chopped

8-ounce can bamboo shoots, rinsed, drained and finely chopped (optional)

2 medium garlic cloves, minced

2 tablespoons minced fresh ginger

2 cups low-sodium chicken broth

¼ cup sake

1 to 2 tablespoons chili-bean sauce (toban djan)

2 tablespoons miso, preferably red

2 tablespoons soy sauce

1 tablespoon mirin

4 scallions, thinly sliced on the diagonal

In a large (at least 8-quart) pot, bring 5 quarts water to a boil. Add the noodles, shaking them over the baking sheet to remove excess starch. Cook, stirring occasionally, until a noodle rinsed under cold water is tender, 10 to 15 minutes. Drain in a colander, rinse under cold water and drain again.

While the noodles cook, thinly slice the cucumber on the diagonal. Stack several slices and cut lengthwise into matchsticks. Repeat with the remaining slices. Set the cucumber aside. Meanwhile, in a small bowl, stir together the cornstarch and 2 tablespoons water; set aside.

In a large Dutch oven over medium-high, heat the sesame oil until shimmering. Add both ground meats and cook, stirring and breaking the meat into small pieces, until browned, 4 to 5 minutes. Add the mushrooms, bamboo shoots (if using), garlic and ginger; cook, stirring, until fragrant, 1 to 2 minutes. Stir in the broth, sake, chili-bean sauce, miso, soy sauce and mirin. Bring to a simmer, then reduce to medium and cook until the liquid has reduced by half, 6 to 7 minutes.

Stir the cornstarch slurry to recombine, then stir it into the meat-mushroom mixture. Cook, stirring constantly, until the sauce returns to a simmer and has thickened, about 1 minute. Add the noodles, toss well and cook, stirring, just until the noodles are heated through, 2 to 3 minutes. Serve topped with scallions and cucumber.

Baked Pasta with Tomatoes and Fresh Mozzarella

Start to finish: 50 minutes (25 minutes active)
Servings: 4 to 6

In Sorrento, located just south of Naples, pasta paired simply with fresh, quick-cooked tomatoes, creamy mozzarella and aromatic basil is a staple. The dish showcases the region's tomatoes, which are famously sweet, meaty and juicy. In this baked noodle dish, inspired by classic pasta alla sorrentina, we use cherry (or grape) tomatoes for year-round availability as well as canned whole tomatoes, enhanced with a small amount of sugar to mimic the sweetness of summer-ripe pomodori. After roasting in olive oil and butter until bubbly, the garlicky tomatoes are tossed with pasta, plus mozzarella and Parmesan, then baked just until the cheeses melt. Be sure to use fresh mozzarella, the milky-white high-moisture type often sold packed in water.

1 pound rigatoni, ziti or penne pasta

Kosher salt

28-ounce can whole peeled tomatoes, crushed by hand

1 pint cherry or grape tomatoes, halved

3 medium garlic cloves, minced

3 tablespoons extra-virgin olive oil, plus more to serve

3 tablespoons salted butter, cut into 3 pieces

1 teaspoon white sugar

½ teaspoon red pepper flakes

8 ounces fresh mozzarella cheese, cut into ½-inch cubes

2 ounces Parmesan, finely grated (1 cup)

¼ cup lightly packed fresh basil, torn

Heat the oven to 425°F with a rack in the middle position. In a large pot, bring 4 quarts water to a boil. Stir in the pasta and 1 tablespoon salt, then cook, stirring occasionally, until just shy of al dente. Drain and set aside.

Meanwhile, in a 9-by-13-inch baking dish, stir together the canned tomatoes with juices, cherry tomatoes, garlic, oil, butter, sugar, pepper flakes and 1 teaspoon salt. Bake, uncovered, until bubbling and slightly thickened, about 15 minutes.

Carefully remove the dish from the oven; leave the oven on. Add the pasta to the tomato mixture; stir well. Reserve about ¼ cup each of mozzarella and Parmesan for topping; stir the remainder of each into the pasta. Sprinkle evenly with both reserved cheeses.

Return to the oven and bake until the pasta is tender and the cheeses on top are melted, about 10 minutes. Cool for 10 minutes, then sprinkle with basil and drizzle with additional oil.

Pasta with Butternut Squash, Browned Butter and Almonds

Start to finish: 1 hour (25 minutes active)
Servings: 4 to 6

In northern Italy's Emilia-Romagna and Lombardy regions, Christmas means pasta with velvety pumpkin and almond-rich amaretti cookies. Inspired by this holiday classic, we developed a weeknight-simple dish featuring similarly warm, comforting flavors. To start, butternut squash is roasted partway, then blanketed in Parmesan; as the cheese hits the hot squash and pan it crisps and browns enticingly. Fresh sage provides earthy depth, while toasty browned butter and almonds replicate the cookies' nutty-sweet notes.

2 pounds butternut squash, peeled, seeded and cut into 1-inch chunks (4 cups)

3 tablespoons extra-virgin olive oil

1½ teaspoons grated nutmeg, divided

Kosher salt and ground black pepper

2 ounces Parmesan cheese, finely grated (1 cup), divided

12 ounces medium shell pasta, orecchiette or campanelle

3 tablespoons salted butter, cut into 3 pieces

¼ cup lightly packed fresh sage, torn

¾ cup roasted almonds, chopped

2 tablespoons white wine vinegar

Heat the oven to 450°F with a rack in the lower-middle position. On a rimmed baking sheet, combine the squash, oil and 1 teaspoon each nutmeg and salt, tossing to coat. Distribute the squash in an even layer, then roast until lightly browned, about 20 minutes, stirring once about halfway through. Remove from the oven and sprinkle evenly with ½ cup Parmesan; stir, then redistribute in an even layer. Continue roasting until the cheese is browned and a skewer inserted into the squash meets no resistance, 15 to 20 minutes, rotating the baking sheet about halfway through.

Meanwhile, in a large pot, bring 4 quarts water to a boil. Add the pasta and 1 tablespoon salt, then cook, stirring occasionally, until just shy of al dente. Reserve 1½ cups of the cooking water, then drain and set aside.

In the same pot over medium-high, melt the butter. Add the sage and cook, stirring occasionally, until fragrant and the butter is golden brown, 1 to 2 minutes. Add the almonds, stirring just to coat. Add the pasta, the reserved cooking water, remaining ½ cup Parmesan, the vinegar, remaining ½ teaspoon nutmeg and ½ teaspoon salt. Cook, stirring occasionally, until the pasta is al dente and lightly sauced, 2 to 3 minutes.

Using a wide metal spatula, scrape up the roasted squash and any crusty bits of cheese and add to the pasta mixture; stir to combine. Off heat, taste and season with salt and pepper.

Baked Pasta with Eggplant, Sausage and Fontina

Start to finish: 1¼ hours (50 minutes active)
Servings: 4 to 6

Our baked pasta was inspired by the classic Sicilian dish known as pasta 'ncasciata, typically served for Sunday lunch and celebratory occasions. While recipes vary, most include short pasta noodles sauced with a meaty ragù and topped with fried eggplant and caciocavallo, a Southern Italian stretched-curd cheese made from cow's or sheep's milk. Often, cured meats, meatballs and even hard-cooked eggs are added to create a hearty, hefty dish. This recipe is a minimalist version.

Two 1-pound globe eggplants	3 medium garlic cloves, minced
6 tablespoons extra-virgin olive oil, divided	¼ to ½ teaspoon red pepper flakes
Kosher salt and ground black pepper	1 cup lightly packed fresh basil, chopped
1 pound penne or gemelli pasta	8 ounces fontina, provolone or whole-milk mozzarella cheese, shredded (2 cups)
1 pound sweet or hot Italian sausage, casing removed	2 ounces Parmesan or pecorino Romano cheese, finely grated (1 cup)
28-ounce can whole peeled tomatoes, crushed by hand	

Heat the oven to 400°F with a rack in the middle position. Using a vegetable peeler and working from top to bottom, on each eggplant, peel off strips of skin spaced about 1 inch apart. Cut the eggplants crosswise into slices ½ inch thick, then arrange in a single layer on a baking sheet. Brush the eggplants on both sides with 3 tablespoons of the oil and season lightly with salt and black pepper. Roast until soft with some browned spots, 25 to 30 minutes, flipping the slices about halfway through.

Meanwhile, in a large pot, bring 4 quarts water to a boil. Add the pasta and 1 tablespoon salt, then cook, stirring occasionally, until al dente. Reserve 2 cups of the cooking water, then drain. Set the pasta and cooking water aside.

In the same pot over medium, heat 2 tablespoons of the remaining oil until shimmering. Add the sausage and cook, breaking it into small pieces, until starting to brown, 5 to 6 minutes. Stir in the tomatoes with juices, garlic, pepper flakes and ½ teaspoon black pepper. Bring to a simmer over medium-high, then reduce to medium-low and cook, uncovered and stirring occasionally, until the sauce is slightly reduced, 10 to 15 minutes. Stir in the basil and 1½ cups of the reserved cooking water. Remove from the heat and transfer 2 cups of the sauce to a small bowl. Stir the pasta into the sauce remaining in the pot, then taste and season with salt and black pepper.

Brush a 9-by-13-inch baking dish with the remaining 1 tablespoon oil. Distribute half of the sauced pasta in an even layer in the prepared baking dish. Layer on the eggplant, overlapping the slices to fit, if needed. Spread half of the reserved sauce over the eggplant layer, covering it completely, then sprinkle with half each of the fontina and Parmesan. Distribute the remaining pasta evenly on top, followed by the remaining reserved sauce, then sprinkle evenly with the remaining fontina and Parmesan. Bake until the cheese is melted and browned in a few spots, 15 to 20 minutes. Cool for about 10 minutes before serving.

Pasta with Sausage, Olive and Fennel Seed Ragù

Start to finish: 50 minutes
Servings: 4 to 6

This comforting pasta dish calls on a handful of high-impact ingredients, packing immense flavor into a simple ragù. Fennel seeds and Italian sausage are cooked together—bringing a double punch of aromatic, anise-y notes. Then crisp white wine, aromatic vegetables and tomato puree are incorporated, adding layers of sweet-tart complexity. Fresh oregano and grated pecorino Romano contribute peppery flavor and sharp creaminess, while chopped olives provide pops of brininess. The ragù pairs beautifully with just about any pasta shape, from basic spaghetti to flat, ruffled farfalle to chunky, snail-shaped pipette, even gnocchi.

¼ cup extra-virgin olive oil, plus more to serve

2 tablespoons fennel seeds

1 pound hot or sweet Italian sausage, casing removed

½ cup dry white wine

1 medium yellow onion, finely chopped

2 medium celery stalks, finely chopped

1 medium carrot, peeled and finely chopped

4 medium garlic cloves, minced

Kosher salt and ground black pepper

28-ounce can tomato puree

1 pound pasta (see headnote)

½ cup pitted black or green olives, finely chopped

½ cup lightly packed fresh oregano, chopped, divided

Finely grated pecorino Romano cheese, to serve

In a large saucepan over medium, heat the oil until shimmering, then add the fennel seeds; cook, stirring, until fragrant, about 1 minute. Add the sausage and cook, breaking it into small chunks, until starting to brown, 5 to 6 minutes. Add the wine and cook, scraping up any browned bits, until most of the liquid evaporates, about 4 minutes.

Add the onion, celery, carrot, garlic and ½ teaspoon each salt and pepper; cook, stirring occasionally, until the vegetables just begin to soften, about 4 minutes. Stir in the tomato puree and bring to a simmer over medium-high. Reduce to medium-low, cover and cook, stirring occasionally, until the vegetables are tender-crisp and the sauce is lightly thickened, about 25 minutes.

When the ragù is simmering, in a large pot, bring 4 quarts water to a boil. Add the pasta and 1 tablespoon salt, then cook, stirring occasionally, until al dente. Reserve about 1½ cups of the cooking water, then drain and return the pasta to the pot.

Into the ragù, stir the olives and half of the oregano. Add the ragù and 1 cup of the reserved cooking water to the pasta in the pot; stir, adding more cooking water 1 tablespoon at a time as needed if the mixture looks dry. Taste and season with salt and pepper. Serve sprinkled with the remaining oregano and pecorino and drizzled with additional oil.

Creamy Four-Cheese Pasta

Start to finish: 45 minutes
Servings: 6 to 8

Rich and creamy pasta ai quattro formaggi—or pasta with four cheeses—is the Italian equivalent of American mac and cheese. The cheeses can vary, though funky Gorgonzola and nutty Parmesan are typical. We use those along with creamy mascarpone and fontina, an Italian semi-soft cow's milk cheese that melts well. A short pasta with contours or crevices for catching the creamy sauce works well—we especially like campanelle, with its frilly edges and hollow centers. We use only three quarts of water to boil the pasta so the liquid is extra starchy, then use some of the cooking water to help to thicken and bind the sauce. To finish, a few minutes under the broiler lightly crisps and browns the surface.

1 tablespoon salted butter, room temperature

1 pound campanelle, gemelli or penne pasta

Kosher salt and ground black pepper

1 cup whole milk

4 ounces fontina cheese, shredded (1 cup)

½ cup mascarpone cheese

2 ounces Gorgonzola cheese, crumbled (½ cup)

2 ounces Parmesan cheese, finely grated (1 cup)

½ teaspoon grated nutmeg

¼ cup finely chopped fresh flat-leaf parsley, basil or chives

Heat the broiler with a rack positioned about 6 inches from the element. Coat a broiler-safe 9-by-13-inch baking dish with the butter. In a large pot, bring 3 quarts water to a boil. Add the pasta and 2 teaspoons salt, then cook, stirring occasionally, until al dente. Reserve 1 cup of the cooking water, then drain; set the pasta aside.

In the same pot over medium, bring the reserved cooking water and the milk to a simmer. Add the fontina, mascarpone and Gorgonzola; whisk until mostly melted, about 1 minute. Stir in half of the Parmesan, the nutmeg, ¼ teaspoon salt and 1 teaspoon pepper; it's fine if the mixture is not perfectly smooth. Add the pasta and parsley; cook, stirring constantly, until the sauce begins to cling to the pasta, 1 to 2 minutes. Remove from the heat and let stand uncovered for 5 minutes, stirring occasionally, to allow the mixture to thicken slightly. Taste and season with salt and pepper.

Transfer the pasta to the prepared baking dish in an even layer. Sprinkle with the remaining Parmesan. Broil until the top is browned in spots, 5 to 6 minutes. Cool for about 10 minutes before serving.

Pasta with Oven-Braised Pork and Rosemary Ragù

Start to finish: 3 hours (35 minutes active)
Servings: 6

This simple ragù di maiale, or pork ragù, braises until the meat is succulent and fall-apart tender, but because nearly all of the cooking takes place in the oven, it's very much a hands-off affair. The tomatoey base is infused with bay and lots of rosemary, while pancetta bolsters the meatiness of the pork shoulder and a piece of Parmesan rind, if used (it's optional), adds another dimension of savoriness. A teaspoon of pepper flakes and a glug of white wine help balance the richness. A short, tubular pasta shape such as ziti and rigatoni are good choices here. The ragù can be made ahead and refrigerated in an airtight container for up to three days.

4 ounces pancetta, chopped

1 tablespoon extra-virgin olive oil

2 medium garlic cloves, chopped

½ teaspoon red pepper flakes

½ cup dry white wine

1½ pounds boneless pork shoulder, trimmed and cut into 1-inch chunks

28-ounce can whole tomatoes, crushed by hand

3 bay leaves

2 rosemary sprigs, plus 1 tablespoon minced fresh rosemary

1-inch chunk Parmesan cheese rind (optional), plus finely grated Parmesan to serve

Kosher salt and ground black pepper

1 pound ziti or rigatoni

Heat the oven to 325°F with a rack in the lower-middle position. In a large Dutch oven over medium, combine the pancetta and oil; cook, stirring occasionally, until the pancetta begins to brown, about 5 minutes. Add the garlic and pepper flakes; cook, stirring, until fragrant, about 30 seconds. Add the wine and cook, stirring, until almost evaporated, about 1 minute. Stir in the pork, followed by the tomatoes with juices, the bay, rosemary sprigs, Parmesan rind (if using), 2 cups water and 1 teaspoon each salt and black pepper. Bring to a simmer, cover and transfer to the oven. Cook for 2 hours.

Remove the pot from the oven. Stir, then return to the oven uncovered. Cook until a skewer inserted into a piece of pork meets no resistance, about another 1 hour.

Remove the pot from the oven. If there is more fat than desired on the surface, use a wide spoon to skim off and discard some or all of the fat. Remove and discard the bay, rosemary sprigs and Parmesan rind (if used). Stir the mixture, breaking the pork into small pieces. Stir in the minced rosemary, then taste and season with salt and black pepper; set aside while you cook the pasta.

In a large pot, bring 4 quarts water to a boil. Add the pasta and 1 tablespoon salt. Cook, stirring occasionally, until just shy of al dente. Reserve about ¾ cup of the cooking water, then drain and return to the pot.

Return the ragù to a simmer over medium. Stir in the pasta and ¼ cup reserved cooking water. Cook, stirring, until the sauce clings lightly to the pasta, about 3 minutes; add more cooking water 1 tablespoon at a time as needed if the mixture looks dry. Taste and season with salt and pepper. Serve sprinkled with Parmesan.

Pasta with Spiced Beef, Caramelized Onions and Herbed Yogurt

Start to finish: 1 hour
Servings: 4 to 6

Khingal is a traditional noodle dish from Azerbaijan. There are two main types: the brothy sulu khingal, made with lamb meat and chickpeas, and guru khingal, which inspired this recipe. The comforting dish features pasta layered with fried ground meat and garlicky, herb-flecked yogurt. Guru khingal typically is prepared with ground lamb, but we use beef and caramelized onions to lend silky sweetness to the sauce. The dish traditionally includes homemade noodles cut into diamond shapes, but for ease, we swap in dried pappardelle that we break into shorter lengths. Keep a close eye on the onions so they don't brown too quickly; reduce the heat if needed and add a tablespoon of water to slow down the browning.

1 cup plain whole-milk yogurt

½ cup lightly packed fresh cilantro, finely chopped

½ cup lightly packed fresh dill, finely chopped

2 medium garlic cloves, finely grated

Kosher salt and ground black pepper

4 tablespoons ghee or neutral oil, divided

1 pound 80 percent lean ground beef or ground lamb

½ teaspoon ground turmeric

¼ teaspoon ground cumin

2 medium yellow onions, chopped

12 ounces dried pappardelle, broken into rough 2-inch lengths (see headnote)

1 teaspoon ground sumac (optional)

In a small bowl, stir together the yogurt, cilantro, dill, garlic and ¼ teaspoon salt; set aside. In a 12-inch skillet over medium-high, heat 2 tablespoons ghee until shimmering. Add the beef, turmeric, cumin and ½ teaspoon each salt and pepper. Cook, breaking the meat into small pieces, until well browned and crisp, 7 to 10 minutes. Transfer to a small bowl; set aside.

In the same skillet over medium-high, combine the remaining 2 tablespoons ghee, the onions and 1 teaspoon salt. Reduce to medium and cook, stirring occasionally, until the onions are softened and golden brown, about 15 minutes.

Meanwhile, in a large pot, bring 4 quarts water to a boil. Add the pasta and 1 tablespoon salt, then cook, stirring occasionally, until al dente. Reserve ¾ cup of the cooking water, then drain in a colander. Spoon 2 tablespoons of the yogurt mixture onto the pasta, toss to combine, then transfer to a serving platter.

Stir the reserved cooking water into the onions. Add the beef and cook over medium, stirring, until the mixture is saucy, about 2 minutes. Off heat, taste and season with salt and pepper. Spoon the sauce over the pasta, followed by the remaining yogurt mixture. Sprinkle with the sumac (if using).

Tagliatelle with Mushroom Ragù

Start to finish: 1 hour (30 minutes active)
Servings: 4 to 6

In this recipe, earthy mushrooms create an elegant, flavor-filled vegetarian ragù with an amazingly rich, concentrated taste and texture. Fresh mushrooms provide the bulk; we like a mix of cremini, oyster and shiitake, but feel free to use your favorites. To boost the umami factor, we include dried porcini mushrooms along with their soaking liquid; store-bought mushroom broth (or vegetable broth) and a dash of soy sauce enhance the savoriness even more. Long noodles such as tagliatelle or fettuccine are a great choice for this dish as the bits of mushrooms cling to the surface of the noodles. Use fresh pasta if you like; to make your own, try our recipe for homemade egg pasta (see recipe p. 15).

½ ounce dried porcini mushrooms

1 cup boiling water

1½ pounds cremini, oyster or stemmed shiitake mushrooms or a combination, halved if large (see headnote)

6 tablespoons salted butter, cut into 1-tablespoon pieces, divided

3 medium garlic cloves, minced

1 rosemary sprig

Kosher salt and ground black pepper

¾ cup dry white wine

1 tablespoon soy sauce

1 cup low-sodium mushroom or vegetable broth

1 pound dried tagliatelle or fettuccine, or 1 pound fresh egg pasta (see recipe p. 15), cut into tagliatelle or fettuccine

¼ cup finely chopped fresh flat-leaf parsley

Finely grated pecorino Romano or Parmesan cheese, to serve

In a small bowl, combine the porcini mushrooms and boiling water. Soak until softened, about 15 minutes. Using a fork, remove the rehydrated mushrooms and squeeze any excess liquid back into the bowl; reserve the soaking liquid and finely chop the mushrooms. Set both aside.

While the porcini are soaking, in a food processor, working in 2 batches, pulse the fresh mushrooms until finely chopped, 6 to 8 pulses; transfer to a medium bowl.

In a 12-inch skillet over medium, melt 4 tablespoons butter. Add the garlic and cook, stirring, until fragrant, 1 to 2 minutes. Increase to medium-high, then add the porcini and chopped fresh mushrooms, the rosemary sprig and ½ teaspoon salt. Cook, stirring occasionally, until the liquid released by the mushrooms has evaporated and the mushrooms are lightly browned, about 15 minutes.

Add the wine and soy sauce, scraping up any browned bits, and cook until the liquid has evaporated, about 2 minutes. Pour the reserved mushroom soaking liquid through a fine-mesh sieve into the skillet, then add the broth. Bring to a boil, then reduce to medium-low and simmer, uncovered and stirring occasionally, until the mushrooms are tender and the sauce is very thick, about 20 minutes. Remove and discard the rosemary sprig.

Meanwhile, in a large pot, bring 4 quarts water to a boil. Add the pasta and 1 tablespoon salt, then cook, stirring occasionally, until al dente. Reserve about 1 cup of the cooking water, then drain; return the pasta to the pot.

When the mushrooms are tender, add the sauce to the pasta in the pot, along with the remaining 2 tablespoons butter, half of the parsley and ½ cup of the reserved cooking water. Cook over medium, stirring and tossing, until the sauce coats the pasta, 1 to 2 minutes; add more cooking water 1 tablespoon at a time as needed if the mixture looks dry.

Off heat, taste and season with salt and pepper. Serve sprinkled with the remaining parsley and cheese.

Index

chives (cont.)

    pad Thai with, 182

    rigatoni pesto with, 93

chorizo, Catalan noodles with, 237

cilantro

    chicken pho with, 66

    Indian vermicelli with, 201

    Lao noodles with, 194

    pappardelle with, 271

    pasta and lentils with, 203

    salads with, 37, 41

    Vietnamese summer rolls
        with, 54–55

clams

    Korean-style noodle soup
        with, 81

    spaghetti with, 159

coconut milk, chicken noodle soup
    with, 73

cod

    Korean-style noodle soup
        with, 81

    "paella" with, 241

colatura di alici (condiment), 96

coriander, orecchiette with, 205

corn

    fettuccine with, 109

    miso ramen with, 84

couscous

    North African chicken, 246

    pilaf with, 215

    salad with zucchini and, 39

    shrimp and harissa-garlic, 225

cream

    farfalle with, 208

    lasagna Bolognese with, 144

    Peruvian spinach pesto
        with, 107

    Peruvian-style beef and noodle
        soup with, 77

    tuna and pasta gratin with, 255

    See also sour cream

cucumbers

    salads with, 37, 44, 57

    udon noodles with, 256

    Vietnamese rice noodle bowls
        with, 46

D

dang myun (sweet potato
    noodles), 3

    Korean stew with, 233

    Korean stir-fried, 176

dashi

    chilled soba with, 52

    homemade, 79

    soups with, 74, 79, 81, 84

dill

    buttered spaetzle with, 245

    chicken and mushroom noodle
        soup with, 89

    couscous pilaf with, 215

    herb pasta with, 20

    orzo salad with, 59

    pappardelle with, 271

ditalini, 12

    soupe au pistou with, 65

dressings

    sesame, 57

    tomato, 39

E

edamame, chilled soba with, 52

egg noodles, 15–17

    chicken soup with, 73

    with herbs, 20–21

    kugel with, 249

    with saffron, 18–19

    Vietnamese pan-fried, 192

eggplant, penne with, 162, 263

eggs

    gnocchi alla Romana with, 167

    Lao noodles with, 194

Maltese-style vermicelli omelet
    with, 223

    miso ramen with, 84

    noodle kugel with, 249

    pad Thai with, 182

    ramen salad with, 57

    rigatoni carbonara with, 139

    soba noodles with, 95

    spaetzle with, 245

F

farfalle, 12

    with carrots and pancetta, 208

    with zucchini, pecorino, and
        basil, 129

farina, gnocchi made of, 26–28

fennel bulb, tuna and pasta gratin
    with, 255

fennel seeds

    pesto with, 113

    ragù with, 265

    rigatoni with, 207

fettuccine, 12

    Alfredo, 143

    chicken and mushroom soup
        with, 89

    with chickpeas, lemon, and
        parsley, 238

    with corn, tomatoes, and
        bacon, 109

    lentils and, 203

    Turkish-style, 131

fish. *See* anchovies; cod; tuna

fish sauce

    Filipino vermicelli with, 189

    Lao noodles with, 194

    Vietnamese noodles with, 192

    Vietnamese rice noodle bowls
        with, 46

fregola, 12

    with chicken, chard, and
        tomatoes, 227

Acknowledgments

Writing a cookbook is an endeavor that is endless, and one of the great creative projects, especially when a book is the work of a team of people. This requires bringing together disparate talents to achieve one well-conceived concept, from recipe conception and development through photography, editing and design.

In particular, I want to acknowledge J.M. Hirsch, our tireless editorial director; Michelle Locke, our relentlessly organized books editor; our exacting food editors Dawn Yanagihara and Bianca Borges; Matthew Card, creative director of recipes; and associate editor, Ari Smolin, for leading the charge on conceiving, developing, writing and editing all of this.

Also, Jennifer Baldino Cox, our art director, and the entire design team who captured the essence of what Milk Street stands for. Special thanks to Connie Miller, photographer, Catrine Kelty, stylist, Gary Tooth, book designer, and Gabriella Rinaldo, who co-art directed photography for the book.

Our talented kitchen crew, including our kitchen director, Wes Martin; Diane Unger, recipe development director; Courtney Hill, assistant recipe development director and cookbook project manager; and our recipe developers and kitchen team, including Rose Hattabaugh, Malcolm Jackson, Dimitri Demopolous, Elizabeth Mindreau, Kevin Clark, Hector Taborda, and Andrew Jennings. Deborah Broide, Milk Street director of media relations, has done a spectacular job of sharing with the world all we do at Milk Street.

We also have a couple of folks to thank who work outside of 177 Milk Street. Michael Szczerban, editor, and everyone at Little, Brown and Company have been superb and inspired partners in this project. And my long-standing book agent, David Black, has been instrumental in bringing this project to life both with his knowledge of publishing and his friendship and support. Thank you, David!

And, last but not least, to all of you who have supported the Milk Street project. Each and every one of you has a seat at the Milk Street table.

Christopher Kimball

About the Author

Christopher Kimball is founder of Christopher Kimball's Milk Street, a food media company dedicated to learning and sharing bold, easy cooking from around the world. It produces the bimonthly *Christopher Kimball's Milk Street Magazine*, as well as *Christopher Kimball's Milk Street Radio*, a weekly public radio show and podcast heard on more than 220 stations nationwide, and the public television show *Christopher Kimball's Milk Street*. He founded *Cook's Magazine* in 1980 and served as publisher and editorial director through 1989. He re-launched it as *Cook's Illustrated* in 1993. Through 2016, Kimball was host and executive producer of *America's Test Kitchen* and *Cook's Country*. He also hosted *America's Test Kitchen* radio show on public radio. Kimball is the author of several books, including *Fannie's Last Supper*.

Christopher Kimball's Milk Street is located at 177 Milk Street in downtown Boston and is dedicated to changing the way America cooks, with new flavor combinations and techniques learned around the world. It is home to Milk Street TV, a three-time Emmy Award–winning public television show, a James Beard Award–winning bimonthly magazine, an award-winning radio show and podcast, a cooking school and an online retail store with more than 1,500 kitchen tools and ingredients. Milk Street's 10 cookbooks include *Milk Street Cookish*, *Milk Street Vegetables*, and the James Beard–winning *Milk Street Tuesday Nights*. Milk Street also invests in nonprofit outreach, partnering with FoodCorps, the Big Sister Association of Greater Boston and the Boys & Girls Clubs of Dorchester.